A Shot of Hope

'This writing is like a love letter to medicine.'
Dr Aisling Ní Shúilleabháin,
Director of the Irish College of General Practitioners
TCD GP training scheme

'In this wonderful book about human resilience and hope, John Travers reminds us that it is in the simple acts that people shine and support each other in the most difficult of times. John makes the compelling case that it is the funda-mental decency of humans that will always prevail, however difficult or trying the circumstances.'
Luke O'Neill, Professor and Chair of Biochemistry, Trinity
College Dublin

'Moving, inspiring and heartfelt.'
Amanda Howe OBE, past president of
the World Organisation of Family Doctors and
Honorary Professor of Primary Care at
University of East Anglia

'This remarkable book of real-life experiences in often the most challenging circumstances will inspire you by finding hope where others might see only despair.'
Tony Holohan, Adjunct Professor in Public Health at UCD
and TCD and former Chief Medical Officer of Ireland

A Shot of Hope

Stories of quiet resilience

John Travers

ORPEN PRESS

Published by Orpen Press

email: info@orpenpress.com
www.orpenpress.com

© John Travers, 2025

Paperback ISBN 978-1-78605-239-1
ePub ISBN 978-1-78605-240-7

Typeset by www.typesetting.ie

Printed and bound in Dublin by SPRINTBOOKS

For Lisa, Jennifer and Julia, with love

AUTHOR'S NOTE

I hope you enjoy reading this book as much as I have enjoyed writing it across three continents and two decades (and that you get from start to finish quicker than I did).

The events described in this book are true. However, the names of all patients mentioned have been changed. In addition, identifying details such as ages, genders, ethnicities, professions, settings and medical histories have been changed to avoid possible recognition. Any resemblance to persons resulting from these changes is entirely coincidental and unintentional. Some family members have kindly given their permission to be included.

Chapters 14 (The longest March) and 17 (It's hard to be invisible) were awarded the Dr Jack Sheppard memorial prize by the Royal College of General Practitioners, Ireland. Chapters 14 and 15 (A shot of hope) were shared online by the *British Journal of General Practice* (*BJGP Life*).

I continue to be inspired daily by the resilience of people who find hope in the most challenging of situations. This book would not be possible without them.

FOREWORD

A Shot of Hope: Stories of Quiet Resilience by Dr John Travers is a remarkable book which confirms his reputation as writer and narrator extraordinaire of the human condition in all its vulnerabilities and magnificence. From the outset, readers are guided through John's own personal and vocational epiphanic experiences as a healthcare volunteer in Ireland, India and Ghana. We experience the leafy tranquillity of an Irish equine therapy centre, and the exploding heat and vibrant colours of Kolkata. In Ghana we watch the 'glowing disc of sunrise', hear the cocks crow, the traditional drums and the church bells, and feel red earth scorched beneath our feet. Ghana is where John describes the 'irony of coming to a hot country to quench a thirst'. For this thirst is his yearning to do something worthwhile with his life. His passion about people, children, family, and issues of social justice shine out. He is on a mission to help those who have been hurt and to share insights into their lives. And so he does.

The book recounts John's decision to study medicine so we accompany him through his rotations in obstetrics and gynaecology, psychiatry, paediatrics, general medicine, emergency medicine, medicine for older people, and GP placements. Through his eyes we are brought directly into those worlds. His clinical vignettes remind us of human fragility, vulnerability and need, but also of human stoicism, victory, fortitude and love. For example, through his accounts of life in the emergency department we realise how fortunate we are to have dedicated medics, whose diagnostic skills distinguish the emergency from the ordinary and who respond at speed to save lives. Too often, however, they do so in intolerably overcrowded conditions, impeded by corridors of trolleys while 'countless more sick patients propped up in chairs clutch their drip stands'. There is the never-ending influx of arrivals; the exhaustion and sleep deprivation of doctors, nurses and patients, awake through the night hours enclosed in this strange world at the coalface of care.

There are descriptions in this book that are heartbreaking. In the maternity hospital we meet joyful new arrivals but also the bereaved; those who grieve for little lives that are lost. Loss can be deep, random and inexplicably tragic, and John brings us into the very depths of such loss with an achingly personal story through which a little baby called James remains in our hearts and is honoured forever.

It is no surprise that John's writing about the Covid-19 pandemic has won the prestigious Dr Jack Sheppard Memorial Prize from the Royal College of General Practitioners Ireland, nor that his account of 'the invisibility of homelessness' has also received this award. His writing is ineffably touching, poignant and potent. The statistics John recounts on homelessness are stark; that the average age of death for people experiencing homelessness is forty-two for women and forty-six for men; that 'homeless people are

nine times more likely to take their own lives and seventeen times more likely to be victims of violence'. These
are the people we pass on the street, who lie in doorways
watching our stilt-like legs striding past their dependence. *A
Shot of Hope* makes visible the faces of poverty, the depths
of deprivation, the indignity of homelessness, the injury of
neglect, and the deep scars of childhood trauma – 'wounds
laid down in the early years of deprivation' – and the adults
these children become because nobody rescued 'the children
they once were'.

Reading this book, it is hard not to weep as we meet
people who have nobody; people who receive diagnoses
that are difficult to hear; people who are dying; or people
who bear witness to the last moments of those who pass
away. John describes the pain of addiction, the agony of
withdrawal, the 'scent of neglect', a woman cradling her
knees, 'raging against her own detox demons' and 'the high-
pitched cries of newborn babies in methadone withdrawal'.
As we read, we encounter desperation and despair. Page by
page, chapter by chapter, we live the life of someone who
cares, and we see through John's eyes what we may sometimes wish to avoid.

Yet it would be an injustice to this book to emphasise
only the calamitous. *A Shot of Hope* is not so named for
nothing. There are passages that are hilarious, that make
one chuckle at comedies of errors and laugh out loud. How
essential to our mental health and wellbeing are laughter
and fun! Nor is sanctimony any part of this book; its strength
lies in the authenticity of the stories and the disposition of
a raconteur who narrates what we know in our core but in

a way that resonates and awakens sensibilities in us that life may have desensitised.

A Shot of Hope is narrative medicine at its best; a paradigmatic, systemic shift from certitude to compassionate listening whereby patients are the experts on their experiences and their lives as lived. The therapeutic power of storytelling has long been established. Its recruitment into medical consultation, into history-taking that goes beyond the factual to the phenomenological, provides diagnostic gems. It recognises the biopsychosocial dimensions of being, and it is rewarding and intriguing for doctor and patient alike. Many examples of how a simple question or extra seconds listening can reassure someone are given in this book, which adds to its potency and charm.

To read John Travers' biography is to be in awe of his accomplishments: his engineering studies in UCD; his work in the international energy industry in the Netherlands and the US; his MBA from Harvard; the success of his clean energy businesses in Ireland and the UK; and his healthcare work. John did his PhD on reversing frailty and building resilience while working in hospitals during his GP training years. He has published two acclaimed books, *Driving the Tiger* and *Green and Gold*. What motivates him? What ignites this success? It is as simple as this – a wish to make a difference. What a difference he makes!

'I'd like to try to leave the world ever so slightly better than when I entered', John once wrote. This book, *A Shot of Hope*, is testament to his achievements towards that. He ignites our compassion for everyone. He looks behind surface to depth. He makes visible those whom life has hurt and whom circumstances have incapacitated. He believes in the power of people to overcome adversity and our obligation to support them in doing so. He makes us peep into Pandora's Box from which emerge sorrow, disease, violence, and death – all the hurts of the world. He lays them before us, but he also releases *hope*. This book is a book about hope, 'springing eternal' even in the deepest caverns of suffering. It is a remarkable story by a gifted writer, narrator, doctor, husband, father, son and guardian of our belief in humanity.

To write the foreword to this book is a privilege; to do justice to John's words a challenging task! *A Shot of Hope: Stories of Quiet Resilience* is a book to be read slowly, considered carefully, absorbed thoroughly and savoured reverently. It is a book to gift to others, and to place in clinical settings, hostels, shelters, addiction centres, prisons, educational establishments and in the offices of politicians who care about health services and the staff who serve in them.

Dr Marie Murray, clinical psychologist,
Adjunct Professor, School of Psychology, UCD

xiii

Contents

Prologue: Festina Lente

*E*arly on Sundays, I spill from my city bed and wake in the safe arms of the mountains. A secret walled garden there breathes lavender as I walk through on my way to refuge. Festina Lente is a riding school for children with special needs and a place of peace.

The children and horses have a unique bond. It seems like a child releases tension from the cage of their body when they meet a horse. Worries unfurl. Wildness seeps away from eyes. Anger, hurt and frustration disappear. The calm spirit of the horse casts a spell, and the child softens as they sit into the saddle. I think it is the gentleness of such a powerful animal that is so alluring. There is an unspoken connection between them, a wordless understanding. The horse accepts them without judgement for who they are.

I lead a pony and a child along a sensory trail. We stop at all the stations. The child leans over and grazes his fingertips on pinecones or pebbles hidden in horse-high wooden stands.

Everybody benefits here. I wash out my week of intense work, running a new business. Layers of self-doubt peel away. Most of my time is spent readying the horses. I sidle to a stable door and feign disinterest. I look away over fields that roll to the sea. I wait. A horse stomps and blusters gently, snuffling the loose wisps of hay at its hooves. Then curiosity and warmth win. He steps tentatively towards me. He blows sweet air through his nostrils over me. I respect his head space and blow back softly. This is hello in horse-talk. The half an apple I produce seals our bond. I brush down his silken flanks and breath in the musk of his neck. I massage his legs. I rest my body against him and bend and tap to get him to lift each hoof, which I pick and brush with surgical care. On slips the bridle, the blanket and the saddle. He breathes in as I fasten the girth and I wait for his exhalation to tighten. I am lost in his company. Every act of this regime is absolution from the week's work. When the horse is gone, I muck out. Each turn of sweetly fermenting dung is like folding away some hurt. I know no better way to unwind.

There is one wild brute of a horse. Thunder has no time for my pitiful sensitivities. He snatches my apple and turns away in disgust when I present a bridle. He snorts and grunts and wheels around into a good kicking position. I jump from danger again and again. I call on Jack, who lives at the stables, to help. Jack tells him who the boss is, but Thunder pays no heed. He has done his long years of riding and wants nothing more than pasture. Eventually he relents, but he bucks and kicks the stable door as we lead him to the arena. He is skittish, pulling at his rope and letting us know he is really in charge. Will he be safe to carry the vulnerable girl who waits I wonder?

Her limbs are curled in tension. But something happens when she and Thunder meet. He becomes a different horse.

He seems to know how this girl needs care, needs to be protected. I cannot know the depth of connection between them. An ease enters her eyes and unfurrows her brow. Her tremor slows. Her body tone loosens. I lift her onto Thunder's high back. Jack helps to place her boots in the stirrups.

I watch them take off. Jack leads Thunder on. He flicks the lead rope to cajole him forward. The hooves thud through the soft peat of the arena floor. The steps are sullen and sure. They have done half an arc when I see the fall unfolding with a sudden fright in my heart. She has lost her grip. Her boots slip out of the stirrups and legs rise askew of the flanks. She starts to tumble. Jack does not see it. He urges Thunder on impatiently. But the horse knows without looking and stops dead.

The sleek black slick of his shoulder stooping. The lift and inclination of his hoof. The swaying dip of his head, as if he is greeting an old friend or acknowledging the truth in the earth beneath him. He gives himself entirely to this moment. There is only one task now. Millennia of human coaxing slip away like sweat misting up from a hot flank in cold morning air. He is pure horse instinct. He flicks his head to the left and casts a glance back, then looks away with knowledge burning in the black pools of his beautiful eyes. All it takes is this, a shift of his centre of gravity, so that his world lines up with hers. There is a cascade of flickering muscles, minute adjustments and feedback loops directing every sinew in concert. A haunch rises delicately, urging her to regain her balance. He reads the modern jazz of her dancing muscles. He holds her in the dance, partnering her every move. Not the predictable movements of an able-bodied Sunday rider but hers. Her unique chorea.

The sheer intelligence of his physique and the endless flow of empathy are breathtaking. He has caught her. She is saved from falling. He gives her all the time in the world to find her comfort. She smiles quietly, unfazed by near calamity, ready to go again. The girl and horse sigh visibly together. Then they walk on.

I walk back through the walled garden as I leave, and fingers brush the lavender. Eyes are glazed in the peace and serenity I have gained from the company of horses. I think about how Thunder cared for the girl and pray that I may learn the same for all I meet.

1.

Burn not like a stone

Her words are faint, like they have travelled for decades.

'Yes, we can look after him. Tell him to come to our house on AJC Bose Road in Kolkata. I'll be there.' The line goes dead.

'Mother T will see you there', my great friend and college chaplain says with a smile of calm and knowing goodness.

* * *

November London is cold and crisp. The tube hurtles me from Heathrow to the city. I clutch hot tea in a steamy cafe and watch workers stream home from the falling shadows. I meet Johnny at nine as he takes a break from his postgrad economics studies. We laugh and chat along the streets. Time dissolves when I meet a friend like Johnny, no matter how long it has been. We finished our engineering degree

together four months ago. The peaceful comfort of friendship is belied by raucous, brotherly storytelling. Even the
pinstriped commuters smile. We duck into a cosy pub off
Haymarket.

'So why are you going?' he asks as the creamy smoothness
of a pint is pursed against my lips.

I do not fully know. I have a cosy job at the biggest blue-
chip company waiting for me in the new year. I could have
put my feet up until then.

'Because there is so much work to do', I offer uncertainly.

Later, as he fires up his laptop back at his student resi-
dence to resume studying, he quips, 'well, bring us back a
parrot.'

I crash on the living room floor.

* * *

Everest melts into the wing of the plane as it dips south.
Arriving in Kolkata is like greeting an explosion of heat. My
airport taxi careers around ancient cars, bikes and tuk-tuk
rickshaws. Bright red, yellow and orange clothing blur as
we dodge and weave. Oxen, cattle and dogs tread the sandy
paths. We broach city streets teeming with tens of thousands
of pedestrians. They spill from pavement to road, causing
traffic chaos. Horns wail and shouts sing out. Rusted corrugated iron lean-tos extend from every building. These dark
recesses seem to be trading huts by day and family shelters
by night. A hammer descends upon an anvil and sparks fly,
a stitch is sewn in a golden sari, an upturned bicycle wheel
spins silver light from its spokes. The evening sweeps in.

Darkness is met by pyres lit in the huts and on every street corner, creating a mystical air.

The taxi eases onto AJC Bose Road. The chit with the fare agreed at an airport kiosk, handed to the driver, has gone missing. 'What paper? There's no paper', he shouts and charges me twice as much. I haul my bag to the curb.

A little boy, no more than eight, emerges from the street chaos. His loose clothes are torn. His limbs are thin, and feet are bare. Rivulets of sweat carve through the street soot on his brow. His smile is wide and bright. I watch as he pulls my bag a few feet to the door of Mother House.

'This is where you are going', he says.

I reach into my bag for an apple.

'No money, no money', he calls out. 'If you wish, you can buy milk when you come out. I'll wait here for you. I am Raj.'

There is a hush in the small courtyard of Mother House. A sister says that I can start the next morning at six. She gives me the address of a place to stay. I have to find the accommodation in the dark but first, the milk.

Raj escorts me to a street stall, where a man squats among his goods. I pay for a tin of what must be seriously nutritious milk powder at the price. I look over my shoulder as I head for a new home and watch the tin being given back into the stall and something small handed out.

Monica House gives me refuge and a hot dinner. After food I stand in the courtyard oasis under a flowering winter magnolia tree. A warm, earthy, lemon-spice, white musk drifts from its petals and I feel embraced. Lightning shoots purple through the distant sky promising release from the mugginess. I have two thoughts: 'What am I doing here and isn't this great?'

* * *

I rise at five-thirty, throw water on my face and shoot out the gate towards Mother House. Volunteers gather for sweet tea, bread and tiny bananas. We walk deep into the slums. It is a place of human carnage. Curious eyes follow us as we wind through narrowing dusty streets, past shanty homes, sleeping families, mounds of rotting rubbish, bodies of decaying dogs and human excrement. Men and women with limbs afflicted by leprosy call and reach out.

A volunteer rattles the gate at the home for the dying and it opens from inside. I am handed a plastic apron. Male and female volunteers split to respective houses. I enter a large, dusky room open to the elements at each end. Over one hundred bodies are sprawled on thin beds on a concrete floor. A long open gutter that runs the length of one side of the room is the only toilet. Peeling paint hangs from the ceiling. I pass to a dim, dank corner near the gutter, where work of washing men is underway. Some men stand. Some cannot and lie clutching their knees on the wet floor. They are naked, shivering, bony and fearful eyed. Those standing rub the crowns of their heads as tepid water is poured from jugs over them. They stand knee-bent, back curled. The perfect outlines of skeletons protrude through glistening skin, open and weeping in parts. There are quick and uncontrolled arm jerks as water is received. Some sit or lie motionless under the cascade of water. I have never seen such frailty.

'What can I do?' I ask a sister.

'Wash this man. Take the soap and water.'

I ask, 'may I?' of a man with wisps of grey stubble and he nods. I feel his bones, rubbing gently over his smoothed skeleton, avoiding open wounds, swollen, inflamed feet and bloated testicles the size of kilogram bags of sugar. Lather, rinse, lather, rinse. My bare hands glide softly. I suppress questions and emotions, focusing on this delicate, privileged job.

'Now dry', calls a sister.

'Can you come this way with me?' I ask taking a hand. The man does not move.

'You must lift', the sister says.

I lift him like a child. He releases his bowels completely. The bloody, beige, spluttering dysentery diffuses quickly into the wash water and spreads across the floor. Another volunteer throws a bucket of water into the mess on my feet, driving it towards the open gutter. The stench wafts around us. I lift him into the main room and take up a towel to dry him. I press it as carefully as possible. He beckons me near as I rub his arms. He says something inaudible. I lean closer. 'Slowly, slowly', he winces in pain. I am shocked that my towelling may have hurt him. I finish dabbing his aged limbs.

I dress him in a faded blue lungi sarong and hole-ridden t-shirt. I return to wash many more older men. Next comes shaving of faces and heads. The blades are blunt. They sit in silence as the razor reaps. Their eyes glisten. What are they thinking of? What brought them here? What lives and loves have they known? What have we all done to the world that such poverty has left them in this place?

I notice a medical trolley in the corner of the darkened room, attended by a sister and a volunteer. I wander over and ask if I can help. The volunteer eyes me and says, 'Help that man lying there.' I find gloves and massage an open abscess at the cleft of his buttocks to release brown pus. I clean the wound and douse with antibiotic powder. There is no gauze for drainage and only simple bandages to apply. I assist with debridement of another man's sacral pressure sore. The sore has been left so long that the trough of skin to fat to muscle to carved-out bone are as clear as sediment layers in an open quarry. The man beside him has elevated a rotting, infected foot. Flies hover and pluck at emerging worms. There are many more very sick people. We treat each slowly.

I join others washing yesterday's garments. We stir steaming water vats of blue-checked sarongs with poles. We strain and press until the dysentery and blood and urine have drained away. Wood fires burn beneath the vats to boil the water. Plumes of smoke waft often through the room, causing the men to cough and choke. The smoke is barely discernible by sight for the dimness of light.

Huge vats of rice and curried vegetables are not that heavy between two. We carry them to benches in the large room, where a sister takes charge of distribution to a line of emaciated men. The men are incredible. They empty back a little rice from their metal bowls if the ration they receive is more than another's. We carry bowls to those who cannot walk and feed those who have no strength or arms.

Another volunteer and I are asked to carry food to a different area of the compound. Near where we set the vat down lies a young girl, about ten years old. She is attended by two sisters and two medical assistants. Both her lower legs have no skin and glisten bloodily. There is a large open hole on her bare stomach, ringed in fungal green. Her two arms reach to the sides, one clutching the underside of the bench, the other grasping a rail on the wall beside her. She cries out in pain. Her eyes kill me. The most beautiful dark brown eyes emit a terrible, innocent, unknowing fear. She seems utterly scared to her core with her body in tatters and four strangers crowding around her holding forceps and cotton wool. I make it five. I am gripped in shock. What to do? I realise that no one is holding her hand and take a step.

'Give us space', one assistant says.

I turn back. I feel frightened. The 'no emotion' veneer crashes away. Every part of me wants to scream.

We carry men to their beds after lunch and we are off. The chatter swells among the volunteers as we wash hands again. We leave through the main door, bolted behind us, into a burst of sunshine. We are immediately met by children, some holding newborn babies. For a moment, I smile at the babies. I want to reach out.

'Take my baby, take my baby. Please, no food, take my baby.'

Their faces are earnest and desperate. One motions to the door behind us and pushes her baby against me. What searing pain must rip through their hearts to offer a baby they love to the imagined refuge of a better life?

At Monica House, I bury my face and drown in the aroma of a fallen magnolia flower. My chest absorbs a swell of sadness. There is so much work to do.

* * *

The horror of the home for the dying is many times worse
than I can lay down in words. Subsequent days are easier
as I know what is to be faced and fall into a daily routine.
Gaunt faces become familiar and weak smiles greet me and
new volunteer friends each morning. I can never prepare for
the shock when I see those who have died overnight lying
in a white shroud by the gate. They are later taken to be
cremated. The first man I washed on my first day is soon
among them.

This is an atrocious existence. Is it better than the streets
only for the food and shelter? Most of the men have come
sick enough to die. Those who get better are handed back to
the merciless streets. The medical care is deeply inadequate.
All afflictions and diseases are in close contact. Tuberculosis
creeps steadily from person to person through the crowded
rooms. Those with open wounds are attended to without
analgesia. All wounds seem to be infected. All wounds are
treated in the same way, with the same instruments, by the
same poorly washed, unskilled hands. That corner of the
room is littered with contaminated medical debris and is
beside the spot where food is later distributed. Many sit
on that floor to eat. Only after lunch, when the men are
brought back to bed, is the entire floor doused with buckets
of plain, dirty water and brushed out.

I despair. I feel angry.

There are two forms of care for the men. The first is care
for physical and medical needs. Its provision is inept and
dangerous, though more than what the state provides. The
sisters do their utmost with scant resources. I realise it is the
second form of care that is their vocation. They dedicate
themselves to support spiritual needs. 'Burn not like a stone

but brightly', they say. They hope to provide solace, love and companionship in a person's final days. They wish to add a last grace of dignity as breathing grows shallow and a human slips wearily away.

I wonder if the men can be reached. Many stare into space or lie in pain. Some babble to themselves. One repeats the same Bengali sentence and rubs his hands by his ears all day. I am told he says, 'what to do when I am alone?'

I feel the work here provides some limited salve. It feels lost in the entirety of the city's overwhelming poverty. Fundamental societal and governmental change only can make a difference. A peaceful revolution is needed.

All the way home, the noxious, rancid, pungent, gritty, heavy cloak of air pollution wraps around me. It turns my nostrils black and creates a persistent sore throat and acrid saliva. I plan to escape north to Darjeeling for a few days at some point. I have heard the sunrise over the Himalayas is a thing of wonder.

* * *

'JT!' a voice hails me. I turn to see a beaming smile.

'Raj!' I call back with a broad grin.

'How are you?' he yaps cheerily.

'I'm fine. How are you? And how was the powdered milk I bought?'

'Good, good. The shopkeeper keeps it safe and gives me what I need each day. If I carried it all, it would be taken from me.'

I gaze at him and swallow the presumption that money had been returned to him.

'You buy more milk?'

'Well Raj, I need to buy some sandals', I say, pointing at the beaten-up runners on my feet. 'So, if you could show me the best place to get them and help me get a good price, I'll get the milk.'

I put out a hand. Raj laughs and slaps five into my palm.

'Come, I'll show you exactly what you need. I'm good at bargaining. He say forty, I say twenty, he say thirty, I say twenty-five, he sells.'

I am laughing. I cannot go wrong with Raj. I motion to Raj to be careful of broken glass on the street, but he treads barefoot over shards without a bother. Eight barefoot years must make for leather skinned soles.

He leads me through winding markets until we find a sandal stall. I muse through various types and find a pair I like. I eye Raj but he shakes his head sternly.

'See, these cut you.' He points to the insides. I peer closer and see a thin machine mould line that would lacerate the skin in time.

When I pick up a pair from then on, I look to Raj for a dismissive headshake or an approving nod, before examining them myself. I settle on a simple pair. Raj winks at me as he closes the deal on twenty and I smile.

'How about you Raj, do you want some sandals?'

He shakes his head firmly. 'I prefer these', he says and points to his bare feet.

Raj and I chat all the way to the shop for the milk. He skips, jumps and hops along. He tells me he lives in a small shanty hut near train tracks with his mother and younger brother and has no father. He is the bread winner. He asks where I am from and what places I have travelled to. He says he would like to see these places someday. He asks what I think about Kolkata, how long I will stay, if I play cricket, what food I like. He beams with every question. I wonder how he can know such poor conditions and yet radiate such happiness. It is as if his cares are as little as his possessions. I get the milk and he walks me all the way back to the gates of Monica House. I turn into my retreat from the city, and he turns back to the streets, still smiling.

* * *

I am getting to know parts of the city well. I start to feel great affection. There is so much warmth, friendliness and goodwill shared by passing strangers. People smile readily and throw a hand to their forehead in greeting. I am stopped often for a conversation or a few friendly words, heads rocking side to side in open kindness. Pedestrians make way for each other on busy paths. There appears to be no frustration in the chaos of noise or milling crowds. Despite the habit of leaning on car horns, drivers are patient. Tolerance and acceptance seem to be abundant. I run into Raj near Monica House frequently. He has been a constant source of joy and light when I meet him. Raj's smile and temperament brighten the day and lift my head. He leads me to a doctor one day when I have a fever. He shows me where to get the best salted lassi, spiced with turmeric, to relieve a stomach bug. His constant smile is not unique. If I smile at a kid living on the streets, they smile back broadly. They may have very little. They may even face early death. Yet they have happy, happy smiles. How is it so?

* * *

The sister is nodding at me. I am at the back of a group of volunteers, and she has just caught my eye from where she stands at the back of the room. She keeps nodding and beckoning.

'Who? Me?' I mouth surprised and point at myself.

She nods. I steal away from the group.

'Mother T will see you now', she says and disappears.

There is a whish of white and blue garments. I am in awe of how small she is. She has a deeply wrinkled face with a gentle smile. She takes my hand in her soft one. She asks where I am from and talks fondly of her time there. We chat about family. She puts her hand on my head. When I open my eyes, she is gone. Now I can't stop smiling.

* * *

I decide against going to Darjeeling for the Himalayan vistas and clean air. I feel compelled to use every day I have here in the never-ending task. I work weekdays with the older men and spend weekends in a home for lost children. Many have intellectual disabilities or severe genetic conditions. These children will never be fostered. We do play therapy, for us all. Every single child smiles and laughs with us. What is going on here? I am humbled by the burning human spirit.

* * *

You know in the morning if someone will die that day. There is something about the distant look in the eyes, the pallid lips, the loosened muscular tone. There is an air of resignation about them. They know it is over and you know it but still you wash and dry them and put them sitting in the sun in a broken chair. The head goes back to rest and the flies hover over a gaping mouth. Later you carry them to their bed and try to talk to them or feed them. Sometimes, they wave you away. They know and you know. Later you pass and someone is lifting a lifeless arm. You see that the suffering is over, and they are very far away and they were just so close. They are stripped and washed and wrapped and other things that do not matter really. Then you get on with the work.

There are times when I walk out of the home for the dying, leaving behind the shrouded form of a man I have cared for; when I look as far as the smog allows over desolate poverty; when I turn up at the children's home after a week and some kid that I played with or helped walk is gone and I do not even have to ask when I see a sister's eyes; these are times when I should be feeling broken but instead I feel strength from the people I meet here and gratitude for the love and care of my own family far away.

My time in Kolkata is coming to an end. I stroll to the home one morning, munching on a chocolate bar for breakfast, thinking of how quickly the time has gone. I approach a bridge over a rail track, where some of the worst slums exist. I prepare for the smells and sights. Then I notice the roadblocks, the military police, the riot squads and the bulldozers. They are levelling the shanty shelters of thousands of people. Owners look on in shock as their homes are razed like straw and heaped onto the backs of trucks. The naked ground where life had teemed is a black, gaping hole. I feel flushed with the disgrace of the scene yet as helpless as those who have lost their homes. It appears that no notice has been given. I see a policeman with a thick bamboo cane whacking the corrugated iron roofs of shelters to bring out remaining people before the bulldozer shears into them. People stand by, empty handed. I ask a policeman why this was happening. 'To clean out the place', he sighs.

'Where will the people go?' I ask.

He turns to the side and gazes away, swishing his hand indifferently. 'To another place.'

* * *

I see Raj as I return to rest at Monica House at the end of the day.

'My home is gone', he says quietly. 'I must move on.' Still, he is smiling.

I am amazed at his calmness. He has a silent wisdom beyond his years. I sense a grounded, untouchable contentment with life as steadfast as his bare feet on the clay road.

I want to give him everything I have, but my own clothes have become ragged themselves. I take off the watch my parents gave me and hand it over. I will walk back to comfort and privilege in a few days and feel guilt at the fissure I will step across.

'Raj, will you be ok?'

'I have my mother, I have my brother, and they have me. We will start again.' There is fire and hope in his eyes.

* * *

I walk the streets on my last night. I soak up the warmth and the energy. Fires burn brightly everywhere. I turn in surprise to a musical celebration. The cheering and laughter of a Baraat wedding procession approaches. Flaming torches are held high and dip and swirl against the night. Trumpets and dhol drums flash and their music rises above the city din. White robes spin and hands clap to the night sky. A white, bejewelled Ghodi horse carries the groom, whose face is covered in a decorative mask. I stop to enjoy the spectacle. Two celebrants drag me, despite friendly protests, into their circle of dance. What a moment, dancing in the street in the heart of Kolkata to Bengali music, surrounded by laughing revellers, bright coloured lanterns and sweet-smelling incense. I spin and the lights whirl and blend with the stars and my body and mind are lost in dizzy rejoicing and happiness. Then they are gone. And then I am gone.

The senses echo still.

I am in debt to the people and spirit of Kolkata. I want to shore up the vulnerability I have seen, gather up the life gushing through holes of the dam against poverty, but I cannot. I promise I will find some way, some eventual, imperfect way to throw my energy back into that work. There is so much to do.

2.

A HEART OF GOODNESS

I wake in one continent to fall asleep in another. Life will never be the same again.

My taxi belts along the sleepy morning coast road. I want to step outside the silent comfort of the car and taste the salty wind. I have been drinking voraciously from the cup of work and it is time for a break. I am heading to Africa on a volunteering trip, my first in years. A young man swings his child high in the air in Fairview Park. Sunshine glances off their laughing faces and outstretched arms. The world pivots on their happiness. My heart aches to be in that moment. These are the choices that we make.

I fly first to London. I use the time on the plane to amend financial spreadsheets with new data, update strategy documents and wade through emails to customers, partners and investors. I munch lunch at Heathrow and meet with Suran, an Indian business leader. We chat about development and energy independence for our countries and map a proposal for partnership in the Maldives. I describe my clean energy ventures in the Netherlands, Guatemala and Mozambique and he shares experiences from across the Indian Ocean. We each listen and soak up the learning.

I dose over France. My dreams are troubled, like sediment whipped up and swirling in a dark lake. I wonder at the path I have taken. I have built three businesses, each one better and bigger than the last. One is the fastest growing start-up company in the country. Do I do the same again? A major international company has made me 'an offer I cannot refuse' to build a new company backed by their massive wealth and share the profits. Why am I questioning it? I have been commuting weekly from my home, stealing away from the people and city that I love. I have achieved what I set out to do. But there is a gaping, longing feeling, like a forgotten promise yet to keep. It is time to breathe and take a wide-eyed look at where I am going.

The bejewelled Mediterranean yields to Algeria's green coastal mountains. We surge over the vast dunes of the Sahara. An excitement rises in me. What is it about travel that opens the mind and heart to limitless possibility? Twilight creeps closer. The night lights of Accra beckon, fired by the falling waters of the Volta. The heat on arrival is comforting.

'Where is your visa letter?' the border official asks. 'Without it, you cannot enter.'

I have none.

Daniel saves me. He talks to the official with genuine warmth and she smiles. I pay the visa fee and walk.

I have spoken to Daniel just once before, when arranging to come to Ghana. 'There is plenty of good work', he assured

me, 'you will find something you enjoy. We will give you a
place to stay.' Daniel helps people find their way. He tells
me about the Irish priest who arrived at the airport and told
the customs official that the bottle they were inspecting
contained water. When the official sipped it and tasted gin,
the priest threw up his arms and shouted, 'it's a miracle'.
Daniel saved him too, but not the gin.

We drive into the night, chatting about football and
Ghana's Black Stars. The smooth highway ends as if a knife
has cut jaggedly across the tar, and we bolt through darkness
onto a road of red earth. We take a break at the home of a
friend of Daniel's. It seems there are no strangers, and I am
welcomed warmly. We share chicken, rice and a dash of
whiskey by candlelight to celebrate an anniversary. Daniel's
friend asks me about Dublin. I tell some stories. His blind
eyes roll, his face crinkles in smile and he shakes his head.

'Man, you love that place', he laughs.

We drive to a house in Adenta. It is after midnight when
Daniel shows me to my simple room.

I wake at four to the sound of traditional drums beating
rhythmically in the distance. Cocks crow. An Islamic call to
prayer begins. A church bell rings. I get dressed and walk a
sandy road towards the glowing disk of sunrise. People are
on the move, by foot or bike. Traders bend to sweep the dry,
red earth around their stalls at the corners of a crossroads.

I sit at a corner stall and drink tea. It is six a.m., and I am
sweating in the heat. 'Why are you here?' I ask myself. 'Why
here? Why not sip macchiatos in an Italian square? You
work hard, take a proper break with friends.' A few reasons
jumble together: I want to spend free time by helping others
if I can; I want to learn about a new country; I have heard

good things about Ghana from an inspiring friend. The truth too is that I am dying a little with a restless thirst that I ache to quench. The thirst is like an unanswered question that can unlock a life. Something calls me to be here to find that answer. I do not think I can find it in an Italian square, dressed like a tourist. There is a sense of starting again, a renewal. I smile at the irony of coming to a hot country to try to quench a thirst.

I jump on a 'trotro' minibus to Accra. It takes over an hour in the stifling heat to cover the six or so kilometres to town. Accra is exhilarating. I walk through marketplaces burning with colour, smells and shouts. Smoked fish, pigs' feet, pastries, clothes and plastic implements, horns blasting, traders holding goods in the air, crying out for attention or reclining in the dark recesses of stalls. Across a highway to a coastal road, through Jamestown, past an old jail to the fishing port. Great, strong arms gathering up raw fish and throwing them on blackened, smoking grills. A red and white striped lighthouse. I rest in shade, then double back to look for work.

I walk the streets all day, stopping into aid agencies and not-for-profit organisations. No one is interested in my opportunistic offerings. I take a taxi home in a patina of sweat and dust. The taxi passes a foreboding looking hospital and I wonder what lies inside.

I feel lost. The whole direction of life is unclear. At twilight, I stand in the courtyard of my temporary refuge, sweating. I watch the leaves of a mango tree dip and sway in the breeze. I listen. I know in my core that things will work out one way or another.

In the early morning, there is calm and peace.

I traipse in pummelling heat on the dusty road to the hospital I passed the previous day. Geckos scatter, then cock their heads to look back with bulging eyes. Chickens scavenge in the sand and rubbish. Past fufu cassava stalls, mobile phone top up benches and hair colouring shacks. Roadside drains are blackened with food waste and baking sewage. I pause at the entrance of an avenue leading to the hospital. Carpentry stalls on either side offer a variety of coffins.

The front of the hospital looks haunted. It is a hulk of a three-storied building rising up out of bare bushland. Threadbare net curtains billow from black gaping windows as if trying to escape. The reception area is deserted. Notices about avoiding stigma and anti-psychotic medicines that are now illegal flutter on a noticeboard. I realise this is a psychiatric hospital. There is not a soul in sight. I hear a television murmuring on the floor above. I walk up and rap on a door. A guard in loose uniform, Fifi, asks who I am, then takes me a floor higher. He limps down a dark corridor. He knocks on a door with a sign that reads 'hospital director.' Anna bids me to come in. Who am I? What do I want out of the blue? What is my story? Do I have a reference and clearance? I am hired before I know it and asked to return the next day. Anna smiles inquisitively.

In my little room that night, I coax huge spiders, ants and cockroaches, which run towards me rather than away, out of footstep's harm. I climb under the mosquito net and lie safe and protected. I slip in and out of sleep, wondering what awaits.

Gentle Natalie meets me at the hospital reception in the morning. We skirt past the building I had been in the day before to a sun-drenched campus on the other side. An array of low, white-washed buildings are scattered among whispering grasses. She heads towards one and tells me she runs the hospital's occupational therapy. Her building has rooms for carpentry, shoe mending, dressmaking, art, games and a small library. They surround a courtyard with two twisting bougainvillea trees bursting with white flowers. This is where patients come for respite from their wards.

We go to collect people from a nearby building. It is like a jail. A guard opens a gate, and we walk down dark concrete corridors. Faces that seem lost appear from the shadows. Eyes cry desolation, some flicker a nervous smile, some a ferocious stare.

Dimly lit dormitories have eight steel-framed beds on concrete floors. Bodies are stretched on the beds or wander aimlessly in a yard with a pit toilet in the corner. A young man gropes along a corridor wall, his eyes glassy and fixed, a hand outstretched and tremulous.

A ward nurse calls out names and men and women melt from gloom to the doorway light. Our group forms a meandering train as we walk from ward to ward, then back through the long grass and blistering heat to our white-washed oasis. It is brighter here. Everything seems lighter. There is an air of freedom. Smiles and stories are shared.

'*Ete sen?* (How goes it?)'

'*Aa ye* (All is well).'

'I cut my mother's cassava. My brothers were jealous. So they sent me here', a young woman tells me.

'I stood too close to the fire and got smoke in my eyes. Now I have bad dreams and tough love, so they sent me here', says another.

'My brother hates me and sent me here' a man whispers through tears.

'I am very sad, how can I fix it?' asks another.

One woman circles the bougainvillea trees. Her bare feet step delicately in the sandy earth. She strokes her belly with one hand. Deep brown eyes are lost in thought and fixed on the ground before her. She smiles every few steps, her high cheeks shining, and stoops to gather fallen petals. She smells their wings of silken white with small streaks of earthen red where the breeze has clipped them from their stems. She shapes them into a love heart in her open palms, then places them in her pocket and carries on.

I move between the rooms and chat with many. I listen and ask and listen and nod and listen. Some draw lions, elephants and colourful birds, some sew quilts, some kick a football in the yard, which I join. The heat burns intensely into late morning, and we sit in the veranda shade. Two men teach me awari, an ancient game with four seeds in each of twelve hollows in a mahogany board. I look up with wonder to see the woman with the petals stepping among the resting bodies and offering a perfect petal to each. She stops at me, smiling shyly, and reaches out a petal.

'That's Frida', the men tell me after she has walked on.

We all gather in a circle in the courtyard at the end of the morning, wish each other health, then sing and clap to traditional songs in the Asante Twi dialect. They return slowly. They are sleepy. All seem heavily medicated. The ward staff are kind, but the system of care is starved of resource. Schizophrenia is the most common diagnosis given to the five hundred patients. It is a default label for a variety of conditions and symptoms: hallucinations, delusions, paranoia, bad dreams, intellectual disability, depression, drug and alcohol misuse.

Patients rise and sleep in the haze of medication. Occupational therapy seems to be the only respite for a couple of hours for the few at whom a doctor nods. The haven of the therapy building is an escape route for those who try. They might wander for days before being found. Some never return.

* * *

I walk daily to the hospital in murderous heat through thick and swampy air. Red dust and black diesel fumes from passing trucks whip around me. Smoke from burning husks blends with the sulphurous stench from a nearby municipal dump. Mosquitos feast on me, despite the trickling deet repellent. I let the sun pummel me and breathe deeply.

I work hard through the day. I spend time with as many people as I can. When I speak softly with Frida, Prince, Kwame, Gabriel or any new friend, I feel a new sense of understanding and clarity. There is comfort and healing simply in being company for someone who wishes it, sharing the path for a moment. I feel alive by just being there, closer to a true purpose.

Frida tells me of her three children and her fourth baby due in three months. She says her husband left for London to lay bricks and send money home to support their family. She shares that a loneliness overpowered her, and she felt like drowning. Her children were taken into her mother's care. Everything she loved was lost.

'But all will be fine, fine', she says quietly. 'I found the rest I need here. I am stronger now. I am ready to love again. Myself, my family, my world.' She clasps my hand, and we snap each other's fingers.

Frida teaches me how to make Waakye rice. Brown the beef, bake the snapper, steam the beans and rice. Caramelise the onions, weave in the garlic, tomatoes, peppers, ginger, moringa, nutmeg, cumin, oregano, bay leaves and umami. Add the beef and fish. Stew. Garnish. Savour.

One day she hands me a fallen petal that has been rolled up. Inside is a crumpled piece of paper. What's this, I wonder? Another recipe? The paper has two pencilled words: 'Love yourself.'

* * *

On a sweltering afternoon, I step mindfully along a shaded walkway as I return with Gabriel and Kwame to their ward. I hear their soft whispers and the breeze around us. I feel the heat soak from the path into my soles. I see the silver grasses sway. There is a peace I have rarely known. The realisation of why I have come flows slowly and fills me. This caring work is what I want to do. Life is unlocked.

* * *

I walk slowly home along the red earth road and stop at a corner stall for a soft drink. I think about Frida's words. Sitting on a crate, listening to African reggae and watching the evening drift in, I throw together a disparate recipe for contentment on the back of a drinks mat, starting with her good counsel:

- ❖ Love yourself. Loving all around you and being loved comes easily then.
- ❖ Connect to the inner goodness that is shared among all people – let this guide what you do and say.
- ❖ Find work that is meaningful and do it with passion.
- ❖ Value experiences rather than material things – appreciate simple pleasures.
- ❖ Avoid judgement of other people or yourself and accept all things with compassion.
- ❖ Forgive.
- ❖ Exercise every day.
- ❖ Eat healthily and try to get good sleep.
- ❖ Be present, grateful and kind.
- ❖ Smile.

I come home late to thick, viscous sleep. The longing that has been reaching its rough hand through the empty shell of me and ripping out strength for some time is lifting. In its place comes a fresh and delicate lick of hope, self-belief, truth, faith and love.

* * *

Up early on a Saturday morning to catch a bus to Cape Coast, a place I have been told I must see. Explosive chaos leaving the trotro minibus terminus overflowing with life. The road rolls through villages of shanty shacks and mud huts. We follow the coast and I watch oil tankers docking at a massive jetty. Exploration ships are heading out to deep-sea platforms where fortunes are made. I buy a boiled egg at a rest stop. A frail woman takes it from a stack of trays on her head, peels the shell, adds a drop of hot sauce and hands it to me. A delicious breakfast for 25 pesewas, some 14 cents. Will she benefit from the oil boom?

The rumble and crash of Atlantic breakers at Cape Coast is calming. I wander through palm trees to Elmina Castle, remnants of a slave trading fortress. A guide tells a group that the port flitted through Portuguese, Swedish, Danish, Dutch and British hands for over four hundred years. They stole six million people. Millions died in brutal captivity. The rest were thrust through a door of no return to waiting slave ships bound for the Caribbean and North and South America. Each colonising nation actually built a chapel within the fortress walls, steps away from the killing cells. Lives were bludgeoned and families ripped apart while the privileged prayed to a false God.

My head rests against the night-black pane of a minibus window on the way back to Accra. The world knows such brutal suffering and inequality. Has it ever changed? I think of the people I have met in the hospital. I am troubled by the lack of care they deserve. What am I going to do about it? Will I spend my time talking, listening, helping and then be gone again. Will I go home, sleep it off and dive back into the comfort of the life I know?

Daniel is closing up the house when I wander through the gates. We chat over tea as insects sing in the night. I tell Daniel I feel I have not done much in the last month here.

'But you are a witness', he says. 'Everything starts with that.'

A feeling grows with every passing day that I have no choice. I choose to make a difference, a small dent in the world. I have a sense the work will be lifelong.

'*Ete sen?*' '*Aa ye*', echoes in my head. I learned from Frida that the answer to 'how goes it?' means more than 'all is well.' It means all is well, no matter what illness, no matter what hurt, no matter what loss. Despite every misfortune, all is well. What a humbling philosophy. Here is a heart of goodness. This is a spirit I want to embrace and support.

Gabriel gives me a full, unabashed body hug. Frida, 'fine, fine, Frida', smiles shyly, her cheeks rise and eyes shine. She rubs a circle on her pregnant bump. 'Fine, fine, beautiful baby. Soon I go home to my mother. Good days are coming.' We smile with glistening eyes. I sleep soundly that night. In the morning, I turn my mind to home too.

Thank you, Ghana, for welcoming me and looking after me, for allowing me to grow and recalibrate.

* * *

Like biting on a burning-hot red chili, Accra is unforgettable. Last night I drove through a torrent of life. Blackness of night shattered by flaring oil lamps, shafts of light from car headlamps, roasting chicken on spits, grilled fruit, people and traders milling everywhere, music blaring from speakers at every turn, dust and earth swirling in the air, shouts and songs, people dancing, laughing and happy, the taxi bouncing through potholes and torn up roads, cutting across and back in the melee of traffic, the heat deliciously heavy and steaming. Now I look out at the damp air at a quiet and ordered estate of semi-detached houses. The roads have no holes. It is quiet, shockingly quiet. Like a red-hot iron thrust into the water, the burning is quenched in agony and pent-up energy is wrenched out in a seething gasp. The iron becomes instantly hardened. My face is heavy with tiredness. My heart carries the light of a nearly forgotten promise I once made. I hear the voices and laughter of my companions. Kwame's clear, deep and thoughtful laugh, Frida's sigh and resigned but happy laugh. The pleading, gentle, lost and shining eyes and smiles both comfort and haunt me. I feel a little like I belong there. I hope I carry what I have witnessed with me always. I came with questions. Asking has made all the difference.

3.

ONE SURE STEP AFTER ANOTHER

The airport shuffle starts at five-thirty. A black car speeds through a sleeping city. Case wheels fly on the polished airport concourse. Every move is choreographed to minimize waiting in security and boarding queues. I see the same reflective faces and dark suits every Monday morning. The energy in the waiting hall is like a rattling lid on a bubbling pot. Fingers on worried buttons, leather soles tapping, eyes flitting from phones to boarding screens, bursting to get on and off this tin can, deliver that pitch, make that sale, close that deal and get back home again. People grinding out a living. It is a relentless weekly sleep-walk for many, the price of golden handcuffs for the big firm commuter.

It is time to inhale and brace for change. I bury my head in a book. It is a school biology book, covered in brown paper to avoid double-takes from my commuting tribe. I use every spare moment for six months to swat.

I sit seven hours of international medical exams in a hall near the London Horticultural Society. My brain is shot that night and I doze through a movie in Leicester square, wondering what the future will bring.

When the acceptance letter arrives, my understanding company chairman says, 'Well, I didn't see that coming', and wishes me heartfelt luck. I love the feeling of freefall.

* * *

There were twenty-seven Johns in my timeless class of first-year engineers. There are just two in first-year medicine. Fashions and names date quickly. Back then, we had to find ways to differentiate. The John who unsuspectingly wore a woolly hat to class one day was forever more known as 'John with the hat'. All his namesakes met similar fates but there was still lots of confusion. The other John in medicine happens to be known as 'John Jumpy' due to a habit of launching himself out of airplanes, so I have free run at my name for the first time in my life.

John Jumpy was in fact the first person I had met on this medicine journey. We were the only two to raise hands and ask a question at a packed graduate-entry medicine information evening for people who had completed other degrees, long before any of us lifted a biology book to study for the entrance exams. We got chatting and, during a shared lift into town afterwards, sowed seeds of a long friendship through swapping stories of the twists of life that had led us to leap into the unknown. We are glad to see each other on our first day back in school.

A professor asks us what we did before. There are graduates of Russian literature from Cambridge, environmental science from Montreal, genetics from Dublin, technology from San Francisco, politics from Bangkok, dance from Bristol and a sprinkling of science, law, physiotherapy and economics. Our classmates have worked as television sports editors, musicians, entrepreneurs, accountants and diverse other roles. Each has taken a winding path to be here. What we have in common is that we all want to be here right now. The sense of excitement and possibility, the lure of learning and new friendships is tantalising. The professor pauses, soaking up the energy of a hundred pairs of eager eyes.

'Medicine has the power to change lives and shape societies. Its science can solve mysteries on a bedrock of evidence. Its art rests in the communication between souls. Gentle words and eyes can help cure too. I see so much potential in this room. Some of you may change the course of medicine. But I promise, medicine will change the course of every one of you.' She smiles and exits.

We start anatomical dissection on day three. The air is cold and thick with formaldehyde. The chat babble of the corridor is replaced by a hush of respect in the room of cadavers. I think of the full lives and loves of people who have offered their bodies. They seed knowledge even as they rest. The first muscle we dissect is the trapezius. A muscular rugby player hits the floor beside me as I work. He had a long way to fall, being a huge lineout specialist. He recovers, a little paler. We carry on.

Our human form anatomy professor is soon a legend in our class. His knowledge is mind-blowing. He guides us through every bone and muscle, every major vessel, nerve and tortuous pathway. He describes their development, landmarks and function. He seems in awe himself as he unfolds the map of human topography. He has shared this countless times for years, yet makes us feel like he is unveiling secrets with us for the first time. His wonder is contagious.

For efficiency and consistency, he maps through the right side of the body. The right shoulder, arm, hand and so on. When he has completed the miraculous journey months later, we clap and cheer and he strokes his silver beard bashfully. Someone whispers from the row behind, 'when is he going to do the left side?'

We learn to crawl before we can walk with subjects such as the 'molecular basis of life and disease', 'cell-to-cell communication' and 'patient-centred practice'. Later we weave through major systems of the body such as cardiovascular, respiratory, gastrointestinal and genitourinary. Learning follows a path of how these systems work, how they can become unwell and how they might be treated. We finally dive deeper into the specialties of endocrinology, haematology, immunosuppression, trauma, oncology, otolaryngology, ophthalmology, neurology, disability and population health.

* * *

It's a dark and windy October Friday night. We are tucked into the safety of a house party at a Canadian's home at the end of a long week of study.

I call to John Jumpy as he wedges through a crowd to get to the fridge where he has stashed a few bottles.

'Hey, how'd you get a last-minute call up to the marathon last year? Don't you have to sign up ages in advance?'

'A friend got injured and I took their number.'

He often seemed to be in the right time and place and charm the path of serendipity to cross his own.

'Bet you couldn't pull it off again.'

He throws his head back and laughs. 'I can put the word out for you if you want.'

'Ha, I'll believe it when I see it.'

His quip is forgotten in the warmth of banter and singing when a guitar appears in the small hours.

I have to read John Jumpy's text twice with bleary eyes the next morning. 'Your registration for Monday is ready to pick up at the race centre.'

The injured runner and a race official at the centre give me their blessing.

Two days to prepare. Too late to start anything now. Cycling 10km daily to college and home has helped basic fitness but I have no running miles on these legs. I do what I think is best in the circumstances. I head to the shops and stock up on pasta.

I watch in wonder as people warm up by running up and down side streets near the starting line on the morning of the marathon. I'd be too worn out to start if I did that. My first jogging in several years is bounding under the 'Start' banner.

I am stunned how the act of running with a crowd of enthusiasts carries you along. I last fourteen kilometres before walking a bit and then running again on stiffening

legs. While others produce energy potions at regular inter-
vals, I save the ham and cheese sandwich I had stuffed in my
pocket until passing Crumlin's Children's Hospital, a lion's
share into the run. My strategy is simple. Keep on keeping
on. My pace is slow, but I know, surely, I will get there in
the end. Story of my life. An official is yelling encouragement into a microphone at some milestone and the crowd
cheers people on. Runners' microchips ping a receiver and
he calls out their names. He yells, 'keep it going Mary', as I
pass. The crowd cheers louder. I am sorry Mary for the slow
finish time, but I am glad I did it. It was a kind of dumb
thing to do. I could have picked up an injury, risked rhab-
domyolysis and taken up medical resources, but it worked
out. Sometimes the best things in life are the kind of dumb
things. Like going back to college and leaving a perfectly
sensible career. In some similar way, I feel carried along by
our wonderful class.

* * *

Semesters and academic years pass before I have a chance to
draw breath and wonder if I have made a good choice. What
I know is that I have the space to make life changing friendships, inside and outside the class; my brain is stretched and
understanding of life broadened; I am living more in the
moment than ever; and I am loving almost every second of
this experience. They say that you can slow down time by
embracing different experiences. We do or learn something
different every single day. It is like slaking a thirst.

We are presented with white coats and told we are
halfway to becoming doctors. The rest of our training is in

hospital settings. Afternoons are spent in a hospital amphi-
theatre where I sense the echoes of thousands of medical
students before us. Teaching covers general medicine,
surgery, paediatrics, obstetrics and gynaecology, psychiatry,
medicine in the community and rounds off with forensic and
legal medicine, epidemiology and public and international
health. We are expected to put this learning into practice
from early morning at hospital bedsides or trailing at the
back of a consultant-led ward round train. There is much
loitering on hospital wards, asking nurses which patients
have a good history to share. We drift to the steaming staff
canteen and share stories of what we have seen and heard,
teaching each other and learning by osmosis. We sit in large
groups where there is safety in shared experiences and
warmth in the fun of storytelling. I often look up from the
intensity of our group chats and see a registrar or consultant
grabbing a hasty bite on their own. Their faces seem lost in
thought and I wonder if there is a touch of loneliness.

John Jumpy and I make a pact to stand on the roof of
every building on the scattered hospital campus and take in
the view from the mountains to the sea. We are waylaid one
day on route to a fire exit and meet Larry, gazing out the
window of a six-bed ward. He tells us how he first noticed a
metallic taste in his mouth on his fiftieth birthday last year.
He ignored it for a while and the oral cancer is now meta-
static. We listen carefully and ask permission to jot down
his medical history. We are supposed to gather histories in a
structured manner for delivery at tutorials. We do this and
set them aside. We are more interested in listening to the
lessons he wants to share. How to be grateful for days with
no pain; how to love unconditionally; how to forgive; and

how to ride a motorbike. 'Dominate the road', he says. What he means, he says, is to fill the space you are given. Do not shy to the kerb where you are in danger of being run off the road. Protect what you value and most of all, value and believe in yourself. What leaves the biggest impression on me as we leave is his quiet equanimity, a calm sense that he is ready for anything.

* * *

Alan pops me a text. 'Are you up for the Hospitals Cup semi-final? We need two subs.'

I can't believe it. Our senior hospital team has top quality. These guys would thrive in national league soccer. I feel a burst of pride to get the call up before realising that final years have just finished their exams and are all abroad. I am tempted to ask Alan how many people he went through to finally get to me, but I just answer, 'hell yeah.'

The coach would not look out of place at the Bernabeu. He analyses every play, every deft kick and every off the ball maneuver like a pro. He is a footballing genius and also happens to be the most down to earth and dedicated hospital consultant I have met. He eyes up me and the other sub, Jim. 'Lads, I have never seen you play, so you're not getting on unless someone breaks a leg.' Jim and I are just giddy to be part of the set up. I am definitely keeping this shirt to show my kids someday.

Our full back goes down holding a leg, not quite broken. Jim looks more athletic than me and gets the nod. I am left patrolling the sideline, watching the opposition wing lumber his way up and down the pitch. He turns fierce slowly I notice. With about fifteen minutes to go and the game still in stalemate at nil all, our right wing goes down and I get the reluctant nod to take his place and mark the lad I have been watching. If I had got the ball more than twice, I would have been found out as the unquestionably average player that I am. But two sweet and lucky breaks are all I get. Our number ten, Alan, finds himself chased and hassled with the ball towards the corner. He turns with the ball at his feet, boxed in. He is momentarily surprised and confused to see his new right wing completely out of position, waving at him in the middle of the box. He is probably wondering why no one else answered his texts, then manages to whip the ball in my direction through a gap among the flailing legs. There is no time to take the ball down and set my feet right for a strike and he has hit it perfectly. I lash a boot at it, and it sails straight at the open goal mouth. Their diving keeper nudges it away by his fingertips, but the spirit is moving now.

My second touch is an unexpected beauty. A wayward ball spins towards me on the wing back in my half. The opposition wing lumbers towards me. I don't have the skills to dribble around him, so I take a punt. I whip the ball outside him to his left and sprint to his right. I've put a decent spin on the ball, and it arcs against the sideline, brushing up a whirl of chalk dust. The fella is still turning by the time I collect the ball on the other side, belt it into the box and someone connects a head with it to put in the back of the net.

Coach looks at me kind of funny after the win. 'Some nice touches, but you were always, always in the wrong position.' Best praise ever.

I did enough to get the call for the final. All the regular players are back from their travels but jet-lagged. I get put on at half-time even though no one is injured. I may be the only sub to ever get subbed in a Hospitals Cup final. I am so bad it is comical. I get dispossessed twice and some fella goes bearing down on our goal with the ball I had practically given him each time. Never a good thing. I take a mental note to tell our keeper, Seán, that I was just keeping him on his toes. One of the best strikers I have ever seen scores twice for us after I depart, and we take the coveted cup. I have a cup winners' medal for my twenty minutes contribution, though I have to hand the shirt back.

* * *

Exams continue to be thrown at us. I just keep taking my best punt at them when they appear. We lose more sweat in the polyester white coats on hot hospital corridors than our kidneys can healthily manage. Months roll by and the learning swells.

* * *

Out of the windswept whirlwind of new knowledge and exams comes a moment of quiet. Peace stretches its hand and wraps me in a grip that I know won't let go. The sun and the other stars seem to swing into line. I feel forever safe. Her name is Lisa. She is more kind, loving and full of fun than I have ever known. Kind enough to bet on a student.

We marry on a bright and sunny winter's day. Our precious family and friends join the celebration. The love we share is more powerful than any words or life experiences set to story.

The meds make a noisy, happy table at our wedding dinner. The laughter rising, the jokes hurling and the mad blur of tie skewed dancing until morning.

I am so grateful for the chance that life might fall into place. I watch the broad smiles on faces of friends living this moment to its fullest. Each of us has left some imprint on the lives of the others. Its collective essence for me is a belief that the compassion of caring for others prevails over everything in the end. That is our class gift. I do not know what twists will befall each of us. I simply yearn for the life-giving spirit of this class to endure.

4.

MESSAGES ON A LEDGE

*N*ature unfolds as it should. But still. If I could exchange my life for yours, I would. In a heartbeat. Sometimes I think of you when I least expect it. When walking through a dimly lit underground carpark; or gazing at birds foraging in garden leaves; or during the *Late Late Toy Show*, when I wonder what you would think and wish you could see what I see.

* * *

I am leaning out the third-floor window. Cigarette smoke from pregnant mothers on the street drifts up. There are etchings on the old sandstone window ledge. Who would engrave graffiti here? It is completely hidden from sight. Yet the ledge is teeming with initials and love hearts, spilling over each other. There is a childish innocence to it.

It feels good to look into the distance. City spires and office blocks give momentary relief. Every breath, word and touch in the small room behind me has been filled with emotion. I turn back to my love. She is resting in the bed. She is pale but her eyes sing with some form of ravaged love that I have never seen.

Wave after wave. Fingernails digging into my fingers. Back arching and her furrowed, worried brow over glistening eyes, quietly crying 'why?' She pulls me towards her and pushes me away. I cannot imagine what she is going through. I wish I could take this cup for her. How can I carry what I cannot know? How can I know what I cannot carry?

The warm August light dies in the city. An orange shaft pulls like an oar through our room. Time flows around our little family. There is quiet again. She rests and I listen. We talk. We plan for the future, drawn closer by our secret.

The old telly is broken. She laments that she wanted to see the *Rose of Tralee*, a talent pageant. I ridiculously act out the parts of the host and contestants from all over the world, making up accents and aspirations for how to make the world a better place. I do a terrible job but she is laughing. Even now, we can giggle. If now, then always.

Midwives pop their heads in and out and offer drinks. They brim with kindness. Eventually they bring a single mattress that lies snugly on the floor between her single bed and the wall. I listen to the city simmer. There is no sleep.

He arrives in the early hours. There is chaos, pain, blood and tears. But he knows nothing of these things. He knows only peace.

He is perfect.

I track his eighteen-week-old fingers with mine. I lay my fingertips to his forehead. I cry for him and for us. He was not meant for this world.

'Oh, he is beautiful', she says. She looks on him with all her love.

* * *

Two weeks later I find myself in the same corridor as that room in the maternity hospital. Room number three. I am in a group standing around and sweating in polyester white coats. We are a September intake of obstetrics and gynaecology students. A midwife is conducting a tour of the delivery ward facilities. 'This room is reserved for women with a challenging labour or who are having a miscarriage', she says. The words fall in heavy thuds on my heart. We carry on and pass the ward office window. A pair of eyes follows me through the glass. I look up to the head midwife I had known, and we each smile tentatively with an unspoken softness.

Lectures are given by passionate consultants and registrars. Their vocations are strong. They have signed up to a calling that ignores the time of day, how tired a body is, what personal or family events are planned. A baby will come when it is ready. Theirs are the hands that greet it and guide it into the world, eyes that note the perfusion, ears that hear the first cries of freedom. Is there a more beautiful moment?

A miracle of design happens in this moment I learn. The baby's heart has a hole with a flap in its wall. It allows blood from the arteries of the umbilical cord, rich with oxygen from Mum's lungs, to rush through and perfuse the baby's body. This is how life is sustained, in every breath from mother to child. At the instant of birth, the baby's fluid-filled lungs purge and take the first of perhaps six hundred million breaths. The little lungs swell with air pressure. Blood rich with oxygen from baby's own breath surges back to the heart for the first time. If that hole remains open, the baby might turn blue from a dilution of oxygen. But a tide has turned forever. The flap shuts tightly against the hole under a new opposing pressure from the air-filled lungs. All in the first breath. All of life hinges on this. What evolutionary genius designed a simple non-return valve to work so elegantly?

My week of evening shifts in the delivery suite begins. The midwives are the greatest heroes I know. They guide baby after baby, family after family. Their patience, care, leadership and firmness when needed are like nothing I have seen in any walk of life. The midwife tends to Mum's every need through the long hours. She comforts and humours her. She acknowledges and assuages her fears. She makes everyone in the room feel safe. I am struck by how powerful nature is. A whole human being has grown in a delicate womb. A confluence of hormones nudges the baby towards the outside world. Usually there is little that alters the course of this powerful journey. I think of the billions on earth that came the same way, multiplied by hundreds of thousands of generations, an irresistible surge of life. I am in awe of the vulnerability of babies and, if I may, the strength of women.

Occasionally, there comes a time when a mum might tire, a partner's encouraging words might falter, a doctor might still be racing along a distant corridor, and the baby's heart is tick, tick, ticking slower with every beat. In those seconds, the midwife will press strongly on Mum's hand and her voice will grow resolute. She will speak in a way that allows no possibility of any other outcome and I am told it is often all that Mum hears. 'Hold your breath and push. This baby is coming NOW!' I am filled with joy for the parents who greet their gorgeous babies. And I fight back the tears of emotion.

Very, very occasionally a labour does not progress as anticipated, a baby's shoulder becomes stuck, or a final push does not happen. The midwives work tirelessly to solve these issues. Just once in my time am I asked to 'press that red button above the bed.' I accompany the bed wheeled at speed to theatre. The registrar on call is scrubbed and waiting. Somebody shouts at me to scribe the timing of events. Within seconds, Mum's belly is open, tummy muscles pressed aside, uterus cut cleanly, and hands are delving into the void. These are among the longest seconds in my life. The silence is explosive. Finally, a pair of dusky legs appear. The baby is passed in haste to the waiting hands of neonatologists. A hack and a gurgle yield to a gasp and strong-lunged wail. Relief floods the theatre. The paediatricians are happy with their early tests and hand the baby to Mum for skin-on-skin comfort and tearful joy.

Towards the end of one shift, some of the evening team are taking a tea break in the midwives' office. They create their own fun by doing a plank competition.

'What's a plank?' I ask.

Jane shows me briefly, then hops up as she says, 'the record is three minutes, forty seconds.'

'Which Jane holds without half-trying. She teaches yoga in her spare time', chimes in another midwife.

I sip my tea until they cajole me into trying. I assume the position. It takes me a moment to hold the pose. Elbows to hands and toes firm against the ground and abdomen rigid. I feel the pull on my core muscles immediately. Within seconds I start to shake. Voices suggest it will not be long. 'Sure, you gave it a go', says someone above me. Then I close my eyes and start to breathe. The shaking eases. There is laughter as I break thirty seconds. A lively, fun buzz fills the room. I break one minute, and pain is searing through me. The shaking returns with a vengeance. 'You've done well, you don't have to hurt yourself. You can stop.' Things go quiet, except for the splutter in my breath. I can sense silent eyes on me. 'Are you OK kiddo?' says one voice. I remember that voice. When you have lost so much, there is nothing left to lose. When the heart is so hurt, the body heeds no pain. I ease myself down when I hear 'four minutes', and smile. I go home a little early just before midnight with a sore abdomen. I know I have absolutely nothing to complain of, having seen labours and c-sections. I hear afterwards that Jane did five minutes before the end of the shift.

* * *

My love and I attend a grievance counselling session. We sit and chat, dry-eyed and stoic. I look across at her and wonder at her strength. This meant everything to us both. I recall that as we left room number three, she stopped and looked around the room. 'I just wish with all my heart that things go well for whoever else comes into this room.' In the depths of loss, she is thinking of others and sending out her warmth. At night, in each other's arms, we fall ever more in love. I hope she knows that I am forever there for her.

* * *

Our class joins the 'grand round' with all the obstetricians and gynaecologists every Friday morning at eight. It is held in a beautifully carved, wooden auditorium, where count-less doctors have passed through for over a hundred and twenty years. Each week, they discuss a recent, unusual case. Something they can learn from. I pray to God my little son is not mentioned. One week, the wonderful consultant who supported us through the pregnancy and birth pulls me aside as I am heading back to the ward. 'We know now what happened from the autopsy', he says. Nothing I hear will ever fill the depths of desolation but the postmortem results he shares give some insight and perhaps some comfort. 'A one in one hundred thousand chance', he says. 'A totally random event I am sure will not happen again. And of course, the hardest part is getting pregnant, so there is great hope.' I walk back to my unknowing friends and bury this knowledge as I have a day's work ahead.

* * *

We step past resting state leaders, fallen heroes for freedom, famed poets and authors. We are blind to all of this. Our hands are clasped. A fierce and aching love for each other and our little son rises up through tightened chests. We visit the plot for our little angel, among all the little angels.

Cold air rushes over lips that breathe in the autumn. On a nearby tree, leaves of blazing russet, auburn, gold and bright translucent wine flame against a crisp blue sky. They are cut loose in a wind's whisper and flutter earthward. A bird begins a song and is answered by another and then another.

My mind drifts to the last time I saw him, in that tiny room. And for some reason, I remember the ledge. I retrace the lines of initials and love hearts. I realise that they were not throw-away messages between young couples that you might see on a seaside wall but of yearning love for little babies born silently in that room. Hopes for some echo of permanence. 'J and L love J.' I realise we are part of a vast group, parents of the fifth of all pregnancies that end early.

I hope you don't mind that I wrote about you James. I think of you so often. The only things I believe in are these: life and love. One is eternal.

5.

SHELTER

I'm soaking up the warmth of the Christmas tree lights at the end of Grafton Street at one in the morning on Christmas Eve. I lean back to watch the star swaying at the top, when out of the palms laid at the base of the Christmas tree climbs Gerry.

His red beard is ragged. His layered clothes look damp, and runners are battered. His grin is half-apologetic, but his dark-ringed eyes are defiant.

'I need a pee', he says to no one. His words dissipate in a mist.

The charity bucket I've been shaking hangs loosely by my side. I had been hoping to catch a few stragglers on their way home from the late pubs.

'Did ya see that?' a passer-by cries out, tugging her boyfriend's arm. 'There's a fella sleeping rough under the palms around the Christmas tree. Ya think the council would do something about that. Bleedin' disgraceful.'

I wander back to the other collectors from my class. Some are pouring a last steaming cuppa from a flask, stamping their feet on the concrete. Some are trying to get comfortable in their sleeping bags on a razor thin camping mat. I start to settle in for the night. I empty my pockets into a knapsack beside my sleeping bag, tucking my precious music player to the bottom. Music through my earphones has got me through hour after hour of street pounding and quieted the sound of coins rattling in the bucket as I shake it. I have listened to a song about October countless times in the heart of December. *'The trees are stripped bare, of all they wear'*, go the words. *'What do I care?'*

Floodlights gape from the ground along the massive Corinthian pillars that frame our sheltered portico. This once was the seat of government, now a bank. Spitting rain and sleet flit between the pillars and dance in the soaring light.

Gerry wanders over to a group of us.

'I seen youse from over there', he says. 'What are youse doin' here?'

'Collecting for the homeless', says a classmate, Jack.

Gerry starts to laugh. He has a missing bottom tooth. His weathered and tired eyes crinkle with disbelief. The laugh gives way to a hacking cough.

'That's for me then', rattles Gerry. 'Youse can give it to me now and all go home. I'll save ya the bother of having to drop it off', he laughs.

'We're collecting for the homeless hostel and here for the night. We're sleeping out too', says Jack.

Gerry starts another belly laugh. 'Wha? Youse can go home but youse don't, there's something wrong wit da. Are

youse bleedin' mad, youse martyrs? Suit yourselves. Me
address to send da takings is da bleedin' Christmas tree.'

He laughs wheezily, starts coughing and suddenly grows
tired. He leans against the wall and slowly sits beside my
sleeping bag. He can't be more than thirty, but his worn face
adds another twenty years.

'Ah no, fair play to youse. That's a great hostel yer man
runs. Give it all to him, he's a saint. The door is always open
to anyone who needs a place.'

'What about you, why don't you get a place there?' asks
Jack.

'Ah no, there's fellas there dat do me bleedin' head in.
Always talking about the next hit. They've been warned
but they'd still sell you gear and we'd all be out. I don't want
to get barred from dat place for when I really need it. And
they do be talking about me when I'm not lookin'. I have da
perfect place now. Smells lovely so it does.'

Gerry looks away to the other end of the portico.

'Who is that fella?' Gerry asks. 'And why has he been
watching me?'

Adam, the coordinator of this whole sleep out and
collection, is shaking a bucket and greeting passers-by. He
seems to have been paying little attention to us but glances
up now.

Gerry clears his throat and looks away. 'What's he saying
about me?'

'How come you're out here?' I ask Gerry. There can be
no simple answer.

Gerry's eyes flit through what might be a painful collection of half memories along a tortuous path that led right

here, to this gaping, toothless portico, where the night wind sweeps.

'Ah', he sighs. 'Me missus Josie and I fell out. Me head was all over the place. I needed space. The four walls were falling in on me. I started sleeping rough. I lost me job as a mechanic. When I went to look for another, they said, "what's your address?" No address, no job. No job, no way out. Now I'm in the rat trap.'

He looks to the night sky. 'Josie loved me, but I don't think she'd take me back – look at the state of me, even me shoes are in bits – but God I'd do me best again and love her if she did.'

We chat with Gerry. He shares a cuppa from a flask with us. He is in good humour and laughs easily. Then he readies to head away wishing us luck for the night and tells us there's plenty more room under the tree. Adam comes up to us.

'If you're willing, I'd like you to have this', he says to Gerry and puts a wad of cash in Gerry's hand. Gerry looks up with surprise.

'That's a lot of moolah', he says.

Jack looks annoyed. 'It's supposed to be for the hostel', he says in a low voice to Adam, then adds in a poorly disguised whisper, 'he'll drink it.'

Gerry starts to hand it back. Adam puts up his hand.

'Please', Adam says.

Gerry eyes the wad. Something seems to take hold of him, like a wave passing through. He takes out three notes, stuffs them in a jeans pocket and throws the rest back in the bucket.

'I know what I'll do with this', and he is gone.

I settle into my bag. Jack retires to his nearby and is still muttering. I stare up the columns to the frozen, sculptured acanthas leaves. I am surprised at how warm I feel in the downy bag. The hard ground is a comfort after a day on my feet. I breathe the icy air and feel the breeze blowing over my face. Distant sounds of cars, muffled voices and the moan of the wind wallow and blend and I drift.

Sleep is like a drink, devoured in gulps. I wake to ice crystals on my eye lashes and the sound of shaking buckets. There is a film of city grit on my face. I dig deep into my knapsack for my music player. My hand searches long and hard as indignant shock rises. It's gone. Bloody hell.

There's no time to complain as I head over to a public lavatory, throw water on my face, tuck into a cold sandwich and start shaking a bucket in the noses of early morning Christmas shoppers.

We break the record for the annual sleep out fundraising. It is broken every year. A mix of relentless inflation and a heightened public awareness, or guilt, of the seemingly never-ending homeless crisis. Every year there is a greater outcry. Every year the crisis is worse. The number of people without homes has more than doubled in the last five years. One-third of them are children. The number of rough sleepers keeps climbing.

The streets are gleaming with reflections of Christmas lights. Shoppers clutch bursting bags and rush to get last-minute presents. Pine scent in the air releases a flood of childhood memories. Friends embrace and wish each other peace. Snow dances from a machine that blows it high above the idyll. A woman throws a fistful of notes into the bucket. She is young.

'Are you sure?' I ask her.

'I have everything I need already', she smiles.

Darkness comes early. We are supposed to finish up at six, but we keep on shaking as long as people are giving. The shutters descend. The crowds drift away to cosy homes. Famous buskers strike up at one end of the street. *'Baby please come home'*, echoes down the emptying street and the singer holds the anguished notes long and soulfully. I wander away slowly, ready to hand in my bucket and end the day.

Broken bottles fringe the street near a drinking hole. Two men in suits are grappling, hurling insults and half-fighting against a department store window framing Christmas scenes.

Maybe it is the cold or the hunger or the broken sleep, but I feel utterly lonely. The comradery of this class initiative has been great, but it is over, and I feel like I am in a vacant theatre, with the players long gone and the last of the audience streaming home. I gather my bag and knapsack and wish a happy Christmas to my classmates. I do a double take as I watch Jack walk away with what looks like my earphones hanging out of his back pocket.

The Christmas tree is on my way. I stop and peer into the gloom of the base, slightly blinded by the multi-coloured lights. The night blackened palms seal up the ground and anything hidden beneath them. I discern two glowing white objects. My eyes search deeper as they grow accustomed to the dimness. There is an open box and torn Christmas wrapping paper trailing from it. New white trainers. He bought new trainers. They are on his feet. And he had them wrapped for himself. I look harder still for the outline of his body. The palms are rising and falling with his sleeping breath. He holds a small box in his hand, still wrapped. It has a jewellery store tag, and I can just make out the name inscribed: 'Josie.'

A hot shower and warm meal await me. I wander home thinking of Gerry and the memory of a song. *'Kingdoms rise and kingdoms fall, and you go on … and on.'*

6.

DAYS LIKE THIS

*D*isaster has struck. An email ping announced the date of my student visit to a general practice to be the same day as our football 'Med Cup'.

I ring the practice and ask Dr Paul's practice manager if I might come a week later instead. She hums and says she should check with Dr Flynn at the School of Medicine, who has arranged our student visits.

I say not to worry Dr Flynn, that if I can come a week later, it won't matter that much will it? My heart is beating a little harder as she checks the diary. Part of me wants to emphasise 'it's Med Cup!', as if it will resonate with her as strongly as 'Italia 90'.

'Well, I suppose …' she begins to say. Just then, she says she sees Dr Paul and she calls out to him. There's a muffled conversation at the other end of the phone. A man's voice is inquisitive, then low and fading. She returns.

'Well yes, alright then. Dr Paul says that should be fine and he'll see you when he sees you.'

I thank her profusely.

The Med Cup kicks off at nine a.m. on the morning I should have been at Dr Paul's, learning what it's like to be a GP. But I couldn't miss this. Sure, there could be many thousands of GP days yet but only one Med Cup like this. A fun day out, an antidote to lectures and a preparation for the more competitive National Hospital's Cup.

Our team foolishly decided to play a warm-up match the evening before. Somehow, the red mists rose and the competitive spirit coursed through us. We chased every ball, crunched into every tackle and ran about like it was the last game ever. For some, it was. Seán, our goalkeeper, hero-ically took a ball and boot together and was in too much pain to roll around. He grasped his chest in a tight embrace and wheezed, 'I c-cc-c-ccc-an't b-b-br-breathe.' None of us fifteen or so student doctors had a clue what to do. One of our defenders attempted to put Seán into the recovery position. Given the diagnosis turned out later to be broken ribs, this move did nothing but ensure unnecessary further torture for our keeper. The same defender would probably have tried to examine his tonsils if it had been a leg injury. Attempts were made to carry Seán off the pitch and the scenario started to look like a stag party getting out of hand. They dropped him only once. Seán probably felt that if this injury had occurred on his way to the match, beside a bus stop of weary commuters, his outcome would have been better than surrounded by the potential future leaders of medicine. He was lost for the Cup.

Our confidence did not suffer a bit. As we stretch on the morning of the competition, despite complaining of stiffness from the night before, we laugh and skitter.

'Sure, we'll probably win the thing!'

One player adds, 'Sure the competition here can't be great, what would med students know about football?' I am still unsure if he realised the irony.

The Cup consists of five thirty-minute games, one against a team from each other year in medicine. Humility comes soberly as we lose narrowly in the first two games and are destroyed in the third.

'Right, we'll salvage this in the next game.'

We pull together, make a few lucky saves. Everyone lays down their body. Barry and Ian racing for cheeky one-two's up front, Sam and Paudie towering over strikers at the back and thumping anything that moves in case it is the ball. The rest of us a melee in the middle, chasing the play. There is shouting and hand clapping and friendly digs to the shoulders. Seán is a beacon of encouragement from the sideline.

I am, as usual, completely out of position. Our stand-in keeper and I are shooting the breeze at the edge of the box. A striker appears from nowhere and chips the ball up over the keeper and rounds him delicately, leaving him arc backwards and tumble to the goalmouth ground. I see where the ball will bounce, foretell its languid hop back into the air and the point at which the free striker will nail it towards the net. I take a wild guess at this final trajectory and launch a dive, feet first into that path. Eyes closed, dust flying into my mouth, unclear of where I am, but glimpses of Paul McGrath in the Giant's Stadium in my mind. I feel the ball drive hard into my boot. It flips up over the bar and there are shouts of disbelief from the onlookers.

We soon give away two converted penalties. The reserves of energy and courage begin to lag. It is a lost cause, and we lose every single game. Yes, we are that team.

Yet, for some strange reason, I feel exulted. Here I am, racing around after a ball, near the end of the academic journey that has accompanied one of the biggest transitions of my life. Laughing and cajoling new friends on the same life-changing path. Beaten on the pitch but winning with renewed purpose. Every single player is sunburnt crimson, exhausted, dehydrated and sore. We collapse on the spring grass. This freedom, this one day away from lectures, tutorials and library, is like a cool drink.

* * *

I cannot walk for a week. Hamstrings and hacked ankles ache. I love that pain. It tells me I left nothing behind.

* * *

I limp a week late into Dr Paul's surgery and wait downstairs in the patient room. He bounds in and calls my name. He is wearing neatly pressed trousers, shirt and tie and peers at me through his glasses. I am whisked into his office. He has not said anything, and I feel the need to say I am a student and not a patient before he asks me what he can do for me today.

'Yes, yes, that's fine. I have patients waiting so I can't take time to explain how things work. You can sit there.' He motions to a chair at the back of the room. 'There's no real need for you to say anything', and he is gone with a bound. I resign myself to being an observer.

So, I watch. In fact, I do almost all the watching. When Paul brings in every new patient, he sits rigidly looking at the screen in front of him. He peruses the history he wrote with great detail on the occasion of their last visit and adds copious new notes as they converse. He asks questions, looking dead ahead at the glare of light. He punctuates his patients' answers with long Hmmmms. Is he encouraging them with an empathetic moan or leafing through the thesaurus of his mind for the right word to type? Every so often, he flashes a glance at his patient but never holds a gaze.

* * *

I am entranced by every intricate movement in the people telling the stories of their ailment. I watch the twitch of lip, the dance of eyebrows, the widening of pupils, the inclination of shoulder, the massage of fingers. This is their crucial narrative. They seem to yearn and ache to tell that story.

'Of all the places in the world and in my life I could be right now, I have come here in search of help', they seem to say. 'I have stepped off the rushing train into this quiet place because I have a story that needs a better ending than I know. Help me to finish it.'

They all look at me sooner or later. They see me watching. Perhaps they think I can help. So, they lock my eyes as they share their stories. I feel useless without knowledge and can only listen. Words from Daniel in Ghana come back to me.

You are a witness. Perhaps part of healing is telling the story, fully, without interruption. Words tumble out like peccant humours from a wound. A reordering of chaos and a return to balance. Every story needs a listener for it to breathe.

'Hmmmm.' Paul is listening alright. He has captured the story perfectly in type. I want to call out random things like, 'that must have been a shock', 'I would have been worried too', 'How does that make you feel?' But Paul does it his way, Hmmmm, without looking. He whips out a stethoscope, a blood pressure cuff or a pen-light and deftly applies them like he is confirming a likely hypothesis. 'Hmmmm.' Almost every time, he outlines a diagnosis long before I have matched a few symptoms together.

He is reassuring. There is a steadiness to his tone, an air of security in his movements. He appears confident and talks in a low voice. Gradually, the tension eases out of the patient. Dr Paul has an answer. He can fix this. This man is a professional. I'm glad I came here. Such relief. No fuss.

Out comes the prescription pad and the pen scrawls with a flourish. Paul almost smiles as he hands the script in a way that seems to signify that will be all. The patient is always glad.

I kick myself for having any thoughts about his style at all. I had agreed to be the observer. Yet, there I was mulling over the way he communicated with his patients. 'You try doing this relentlessly for thirty years', I tell myself. What does it matter? Observe, don't judge. He has his way, and it works for him and seems to work for his patients. You may someday have your way, not better, not worse, just different.

He brings an elegant older lady into his office. She is dressed in a lilac skirt and pale silk blouse. She looks frail, tired and disconsolate as she dabs a tissue to her nose. Her silver hair is radiant. She takes a seat beside his desk. He busies himself with clicking into her file.

'How are you doing Maria?'

She raises her eyes to search the side of his face. Her lips form to say a word that remains secret. She is quiet for a moment and retreats slightly in her seat. She sighs tentatively.

'Not very well', she whispers. 'It has only been three months. I'm still getting used to it.' Her gaze drifts. The pallor of her face shifts and clouds. Her eyes well up.

Paul glances at her and hums quietly. 'Yes', he says. He resumes his perusal of her history.

'I came to ask you about my side', she says. She moves her thin hand like a ghost and silently touches her fifth and sixth ribs on her right side.

'Hmmmm.'

He asks the normal questions. She obliges, describing the ailment in detail. He asks her to stand up, remove her blouse and perform various movements. He palpates. He listens to her lungs and heart.

'Well', he says finally, 'I think we should arrange an X-ray for you just to have a look.'

'Oh', she laments gently. 'An X-ray did not find what Marty had.'

'Well, it might be entirely different. It is just to get a better picture.'

'It didn't show Marty's tumour and by the time we found out, we had two weeks.' Her eyes well again and she sits down bereft of energy.

'I miss him terribly.'

'Hmmmm.'

I want to step across and embrace her.

'Yes, so I will write the letter of referral and the results will come back to me so you should make an appointment with me again in about three weeks.'

'Maybe he is calling me.'

'It's just to get some clarity.'

Silence hangs as Paul types and Maria stares at the floor. It seems like a couple of minutes pass. We could all be sitting in separate rooms. I feel an overwhelming wish to reach across the divide. I dig and turn sods of ideas. Paul appears to be wrapping up his file update.

'Your hair is lovely', I say hurriedly.

She looks a little surprised and places a hand to the back of her head.

'Did you get it done recently?'

'Ooh, yes just this morning.' She smiles bashfully. 'Well, I got it set, you know … just to cheer myself up.'

'It looks great', I say.

Paul looks between us, as if to check if we are ready now. He gets up and motions Maria to the door.

'I'll see you in three weeks', he tells her.

Maria leaves quietly and Paul goes back to screen scrolling for his next patient.

'Will I ever last thirty years?' I wonder.

7.

INTERNING

$\mathcal{I}$ hold her in my arms until she falls asleep each night. I feel her warmth of surging life against my chest. The peace from her tiny two-week-old body can save the world. I place her delicately into her cot and watch the rise and fall of her breath and the calmness in her face.

I wonder with hope at the experiences that might line her life's path, the creases that might grace her face. I pray that she may be loved at every moment – in days of growth, in wondrous independence and in times of care. Will someone, someday, meet her as I meet older women in my work? Will they realise that in this moment, she was perfect?

* * *

I start my medical internship at a hospital in the leafy south city just days after she is born.

I realise they are trying to kill me after a few days. Well, just deprive me of rest and food. I am rostered for the first weekend 'call' after the July handover. 'Call' is a throwback to days when I imagine doctors reclining on library couches waiting for an occasional call to a ward. The July handover is when most non-consultant hospital doctors switch roles and locations. It takes days to get to grips with new responsibilities and software. There is fumbling and chaos. Nurses carry the extra load of keeping people alive. Who are the sole two doctors left to manage every medical issue of every patient in the entire hospital on the first weekend after handover? Clara and I, only weeks after graduation.

There is one pager to call for all medical support in the twenty-two-ward, six-hundred-bed public hospital. Clara and I agree that one of us will hold the pager to field emergency calls, while the other sweeps the hospital, ward by ward, to complete jobs posted on whiteboards. We can swap roles every two hours. There are two medical senior house officers and one registrar working in the emergency department. They are available to support us in theory. In practice, they are pushed to their limits admitting and stabilizing new patients and have let it be known that we should call them as an absolute last resort. Everyone carries a dedicated pager that will go off in the event of a cardiac arrest anywhere in the hospital. We must also manage any arrests in the adjacent, two-hundred-and-forty-bed private hospital.

The Pavlovian sting of the medical pager bleeping every few minutes keeps the adrenalin pumping. It takes full concentration not to jump when it goes off while holding a needle in a sick patient's radial artery. I jam an arterial blood sample into a blood gas analysis machine with one hand and answer the bleep with the other. The machine announces it has failed and needs to shut down for a clean as a nurse relays the need for an emergency review at the other end of the hospital. I race up two flights of stairs to the next available blood gas machine and the pager bleeps twice more.

Pager calls are wildly variable. A patient with sudden chest pain makes me run. A request to rewrite prescriptions in a fresh booklet makes me groan. I place so many venous cannulas that I can no longer meet anyone without my eyes drifting over the veins of their forearms and hands to assess how plump and forgiving they are.

I speed through an online video to remind myself how to insert a urinary catheter as I gather equipment in a storeroom and grapple with the task seconds later. We have watched and learned while we were students but the first time for every independent act is now. Instincts are honed quickly.

I manage a high blood potassium that might kick off a fatal heart arrythmia; adjust insulin after a dangerously low blood sugar event; assess lack of bowel movement post infection; write two discharge letters (why is the most junior medic, who has never seen the patients, writing key information for ongoing care to their GPs?); chart warfarin; measure cortisol levels; examine a rash; investigate an oxygen desaturation; order a chest X-ray; diagnose pneumonia and prescribe treatment; support a psychiatric patient to eat again; run a cannula through a nose and into a stomach and request an X-ray to make sure I have not passed it into the brain or lungs; take blood cultures; evaluate a collapse; appraise ECGs; and review a seizure.

We have no time to reflect on what we are doing. Some might suggest that deep-end learning is the making of a real-world doctor. I feel the ethics are questionable from a patient perspective. Why are there only two medical doctors covering an entire hospital? Why are those two doctors not a wet week in the job? Where is the experienced senior cover? Why is there no consultant on site? I realise that medical expertise is a Monday-to-Friday, nine-to-five service in this publicly funded national hospital, while illness is relentless. I see that nursing care is the backbone of healthcare. It is the only consistent and round-the-clock service.

I answer a bleep and a nurse asks me to pronounce. It takes me a moment to understand what she means. There is only silence in the small room. I meet the lady's daughter. She has minded her mother through a long illness, petting her brow, holding her hand. She holds her hand now and looks up at me, broken-hearted. She leaves the room for a moment, and I am alone with the stillness. I listen to the silence through a stethoscope on her chest, shine a light and close her eyes. The deathly quiet is much more than the absence of sound. It is part of a final crescendo, like the relief after a wave pummels all its energy on a shore. 'This life was full', it says. The surge is done. Peace floods her face.

There is a gathering of relatives in the little corridor outside the door. I make a line for the daughter and offer her my hand and condolences. I am confirming what she already knows, what they all already know. But at this moment, when her hand is gripped, all the expectant heads drop, and shoulders sag a little. I am a stranger. Yet I have performed this ancient, privileged ritual for this family on this day. The grieving begins. Each finds a path to shake my hand and give thanks. It has very little to do with me, I think. They are shaking the hand as passage to shifted futures.

I mute bleep after bleep, then back away from this pivot in their lives and start running again. We are charging towards seventy bleeps in the first twelve hours, on top of the posted jobs in the wards. Then it goes off.

A burst of panic is quelled by my pounding steps echoing along empty corridors. A door is flung open and Clara joins as we race towards the destination crackling from the pager. The Emergency Department (ED) doctors have dropped everything, and I am stunned to see a wide-eyed surgical intern in theatre scrubs join the fray. Some take the dodgy lift as I double up three flights of stairs.

Five frightened patients watch as curtains are spun around the sixth bed in the ward. An anaesthetics registrar from theatre calls the shots. I am on the chest. A frail man looks utterly at rest and his skin is cool. He may have passed away in his sleep before a nurse found him on her rounds and hit an arrest button. We follow our resuscitation training in the absence of an end-of-life directive from this man. I apply thirty compressions four times, interspersed with bag-mask breaths from Clara. The senior house officers try for venous cannulation to offer life-renewing adrenalin. The registrar calls it soon. Her experience and sense of respect transcend our methodical actions. I pick up the scattered blankets and discarded equipment wrappers from around the bed and wish this man peace. Clara and I walk away, sweating and drained. The sensations of compressing this man's ribcage are still running through my arms and hands. There is no debrief. Just each other's shocked and knowing company.

The bleeps have been stacking up and we do our best to clear them. I pass a room on Monica Ward and notice the name on the oncology patient chart. Larry. I long to drop in and see how he is doing and say thanks for his advice to 'dominate the road', which I recall daily on my bicycle commute. A ward nurse tells me that he has been moved to a single room for end-of-life comfort and is trying a last-gasp experimental treatment from the US. My bleep goes off and I have to rush away with words left unspoken.

I dart down to the basement for a short cut and race along dark corridors with steaming pipes. Above me the building groans. An aching drone of machines whirring and beeping, people washing and dressing, bleeding and vomiting, healing and wasting, turning restlessly in beds, taking first post-surgical shuffling steps and last breaths. Waves are exchanged with catering staff preparing dinners, porters wheeling beds, the security team rounding, nurses huddled over charts – the lifeblood of the hospital, all working to get people safely home again.

The night interns will be arriving for handover soon. This is a revelation I never considered when signing up for this vocation. Nightshift. Of course, it was always there. Of course, someone has to cover the calls at night; the more junior, the more calls; the more learning. But nightshift was not 'mentioned in the brochure'. I chuckle to myself. That is ok. Bring it on. Juniors frontloaded with responsibility, long hours, minimal resources and working through the night. If this is what it takes to grow, I will swallow it up, and anything more that is thrown at me. I have a window to a new world. An opportunity to help others. It is fascinating and daunting and life-enhancing. Not all of it makes sense.

More advanced junior doctor colleagues are mobilizing to negotiate a work shift maximum of twenty-four hours, down from thirty-six. Perhaps I can help shift the needle in the future.

Clara laughs as we chat back in the resident doctors' room at handover. She tells me senior doctors forget the trauma of their training when they have progressed through the ranks. We might be just like them in no time, Clara jokes. What is best for patients though, we wonder together.

I jump at the sound of the bleep going off as I leave the res room for a final visit to Monica Ward to say farewell to Larry. My heart rate settles as I realize the pager is now in the hands of a new night intern. He stares at it for the first time, unaware of what the night will bring. I shout that I will see him early Sunday morning for handover again. I look out through a window for the first time that day and see the stars rising. I will make it home just in time to rock my daughter to sleep.

8.

TIME TO GROW

*I*t is time to choose. I have been accepted on both the general practice and medical specialist training schemes. If I were younger and rash again, I might throw myself headlong into a medical specialty and race down a path to cardiology. The heart is iconic. It pumps life force through us, courses with astonishing electricity and is the imagined, if misplaced, home of love. I felt drawn to cardiology in student days: listening intently to lectures from cutting edge consultants and spending summer electives with them. I stood for hours beside one inspiring cardiologist, Joe, sweating under protective lead gowns during electrophysiology surgery, burning out pathways for aberrant electrical currents causing atrial fibrillation in the muscle of the heart, and soaking up the knowledge of his mentoring. I asked if he had gathered data on all the ablations he had done. I trawled through the numbers after hours, searching for patterns and calculating correlations. We uncovered a whole new way to look at scars in the heart's fibres caused by life's wear and tear based on this data and named it the Dublin classification at an international conference in Nice. A good start. I am tempted to follow this path. It would mean a further ten years of training, hospital night shifts and international fellowships.

There is something else on offer. The diversity, humility and patience that comes with a general practice. The health of an open mind, not knowing who will walk through the door with what medical issue. The recurrent joy of greeting new babies to new centenarians. The privilege of listening. The confidence of their greatest secrets, fears and hopes. The comfort and equality of working in the community. The autonomy of setting your own hours, running your own service. The relaxed collegiality and dissolution of hierarchy. The longevity of getting to know and care for patients, whole families and generations for the length of our shared lives. The life-long learning. The opportunity to offer solace in moments of despair or grief. The chance to help someone unburden a worry and get back to reaching their potential. Most of all, witnessing the relief in a person when they take a sure step on the path from illness to wellness. I believe there can be a shift in energy in the core of a person between entering and leaving a consultation room. With care, they leave stronger and better; a weight lifted, a fear assuaged, an insight gained, a remedy started. If I could be paid with a small commission of that energy, I would have more than enough.

* * *

Lisa and I are blessed with a second daughter. I learn so much from her. Her strength swells with each passing moment. It appears to grow with every gentle touch, kiss, encouraging word and song, with every time our eyes meet, and every loving care that we four share. It seems to grow also when her eyes turn to a flicker of sunlight through leaves, when she listens to the sounds of the city streets, or Atlantic waves in our Kerry retreat, from the scents and suckle and grasp of the unexplored world. That is how the love in our hearts and the energy from every living thing around us appear to connect. They share in the making of sustenance for growth. I do not want to miss these moments. I ask my two daughters what path I should take one night and listen to their sleeping breaths. I listen to Lisa's wisdom.

* * *

I choose general practice. So does John Jumpy. We are excited to share a four-year journey on the training scheme after our internship. It will involve six hospital rotations in general medicine; emergency medicine; psychiatry; medicine for older people; obstetrics and gynaecology; and paediatrics; and a year in each of two general practice surgeries. We are safe again on the path of learning and growth.

9.

RUN ALL NIGHT

*T*he garda at the barricade shouts at me, 'Ya can't get through, it's a mess.'

'I'm on-call at the hospital emergency department and have to get over there.' She throws an eye over me and my battered bicycle. A resonant flash of frontline empathy loosens the fierceness in her face. 'Go on. You might just make it. You'll have a busy one I'd say.' She lifts the steel barrier. 'Thanks a mill, no more than yourself I'd say', and I'm gone with a wave.

This well-beaten bike commute works on any other day but today I have misjudged it. I had wanted to soak up just a few moments of St Patrick's Day atmosphere before getting sucked into the dark shaft of an endless night in the emergency department.

I bomb down Camden Street and get swallowed by a river of colour. I drag my hazard of a bike through the shuffling crowd but when the parade crosses my path I am snookered. Grinning giants leer above me. Batons flung into the ice-blue sky flash in the sun. Hypnotic drumbeats cut through the air. The percussion intensity soars and clutches my heart as marching bands approach. I am part of this effervescent surge of colour and music. I try absorbing it all to carry it with me, and back away wondering if I would see any of these revellers later, lying on a trolley, literally trollied.

I peg it through littered back streets and chase down the end of the parade, then cut around it and head north through the city. Over the river Liffey at Butt Bridge to the music of a DART train rattling on an overhead track. A reflection of Liberty Hall wallows in the river's dank waters. Whispers of the Wicklow Mountains and secrets from ancient black bogs, entwined with the city's sweat, lap against discarded bicycles and traffic cones in the alginous mud of low tide. The briny, unctuous smell and screams of seagulls fighting for a foothold on crap-capped masts spur me on. 'I love this city', I think as I make up time and the sweat pours out of me along Gardiner Street.

'Your mother does not work here', reads the scrawl on a poster. 'Put your used scrubs in the bin provided, not on the floor.' The changing room is a shambles. Used scrubs, old runners and last week's forgotten sandwiches have been kicked into a corner. Lockers from people who worked here years ago and have absconded with keys remain forever shut and about twenty coats cling to the four hooks on the back of the door. I throw on clean scrubs, give my forearms and hands a good wash and head out to the Emergency Department (ED) floor.

I feel a stab from the chaos. The air is thick and hot. It resounds with groans and shouts. We have run out of beds again. Multiple overflow trolleys block walkways and count-less more sick patients are propped up in chairs clutching their drip stands. Someone had peddled me a line that it was the second busiest ED in the world, after Sao Paulo. This might be put to the test tonight. It feels like the busiest.

Emergency doctors finishing their shifts are typing up final notes with drained faces in the sanctity of the nurses' station. Ollie is my co-senior house officer (SHO) for the rest of the day and night. It is the second of a run of five night shifts. We know we are in the trench together and have each other's backs.

'What reg is on?' I ask.

'Ted.'

'Ah fantastic.'

This ED job expects you to hit the ground running from day one. The specialist registrars carving a career in ED medicine are fully supportive and the nurses are second to none. Although the ailments change, the approach to history-taking and examination is consistent. People are triaged on arrival by a nurse. If they do not require resuscitation, they return in varying degrees of discom-fort to plastic chairs in the teeming waiting room. Their triage notes are placed in pink or blue envelopes, labelled category one, two or three, depending on severity and left at the nurses' station. You pick up an envelope at the front of the pile, note the time since triage, which could be from one to an appalling twelve hours, read the contents, then call for them in the waiting room on the chance they are still there. Assessment starts with how the person looks and moves on meeting them. You take a history, examine appropriately and form a working diagnosis, then order tests to confirm or refine this. You draw blood samples, complete an ECG or order X-rays and other scans as indicated. You pick up several more envelopes while waiting for results and care for four or five patients at any one time. Some have a non-emergency diagnosis, receive treatment and can be discharged home. Some are acutely unwell and need stabilisation and in-patient care. They are referred to medics or surgeons for hospital admission and ongoing care after initial treatment and investigative work-up.

There are typically four senior house officers and two to three registrars working during the day, with just two and one respectively at night. A publicly paid consultant may or may not join the floor during the day or may or may not be seeing patients in the private hospital across the street, within running distance. On a busy shift, it is all hands-on deck working with the resuscitation and category one patients, creating a long waiting time for category two patients and God help category three.

I get up and running with a category two envelope that has been waiting a long time. It is pink. I unfold the single page inside. My eyes widen as I read. "Marianne B; 28-year-old woman; says she was held hostage for four hours with a meat cleaver; alleges she was forced to ingest an unknown brown substance; to be assessed for poisoning."

'Three hours, she's been waiting for three hours', I think in disbelief. I scan the recorded vital signs, which were all normal, walk straight to the waiting room and call out her name. No answer. I go to the triage nurse.

'Any sign of this lady?' I ask.

'Ah she's gone. She was fighting with everyone, told security to go f… themselves and walked out.'

I rush through the nearby doors to the street. She is sitting on a kerb, clutching her knees. She pulls back a hood to reveal a tear-stained face when I call her name. She agrees to join me, and I listen to her awful story in a grimy assessment room with a nurse colleague. We offer her counselling and social supports and help in working with the gardaí. The ED is overflowing, and she prefers to return to the melee of the waiting room while I send bloods and urine sample to the labs.

* * *

I look at the growing pile of envelopes with unknown issues waiting to be seen. What the hell were the category ones like if this woman got bumped to category two? I pick up a blue category one envelope.

A staff nurse who has spotted this particular envelope in my hand says, 'see that guy and get him out of here.'

'Why's that?' I ask as I scan key words. "Mark H; 29-year-old; abdominal pain; vomiting; vitally stable."

'He's complaining too much. He's pale but fine. Quick review and get him home.'

I wander down the corridor towards the waiting room thinking that the system is even more messed up if he was put in category one.

Mark looks awful. He is pale and clammy, and his grimace reflects what I sense is real pain. Instinct presses me to glance again at the ECG that the triage nurse had kindly done. It showed normal sinus rhythm. His girlfriend is deadly serious. Her body language has the tense calm of a tightly strung bow and there is fearful intensity in her eyes. She knows this man in all shades of character and her anxiety is a telling sign.

His first words are to say thanks for seeing him. Not about how awful he feels or how long he has waited but that he is grateful. I ask about his pain. He describes sudden onset central abdominal pain, starting about three hours ago, sharp, 'seven out of ten' in intensity, no radiation, relieved by large vomits on two occasions about an hour apart. Recent bowel movement though no diarrhoea, no urinary symptoms, no history of ingesting anything strange and his girlfriend has eaten everything he has, no sick contacts. He had his appendix out fifteen years previously and had no other relevant medical or surgical history, not on regular medicines, no allergies, not a big drinker, non-smoker, no relevant family history. This guy was previously well.

His vital signs are all within normal ranges. I ask permission to examine. I have been taking mental notes about his hands, eyes and mouth throughout our history taking. Nothing else has appeared abnormal so far. I look into his eyes and press my hands across his abdomen in nine different places. He maintains the same strained look with no sudden grimace, no wince, no hand raised to guard against my touch. I go back and press harder. I feel for spleen, kidneys, liver and any lumps. Breathe in, breathe out. I listen by stethoscope and wait for the faint gurgle. I start to release a little tension. Everything is as it should be. Soft and non-tender, no flank pain, no hernias, no organs larger than expected. Cardiovascular and respiratory exams are normal.

He says he realises there may be others sicker than him in ED and thanks me for taking time with him. His girlfriend remains concerned. I chat with him in an open, transparent way. He agrees that a gastroenteritis bug has to be high on that list of differentials. I take a full set of blood samples and order chest and abdominal X-rays, despite the seemingly low indication. I start some slow intravenous fluids, say that we will keep a close eye and offer some of those cardboard hats in case he needs to vomit again. He looks at a nurse setting up a drip and asks how her shift has gone so far. He seems to think only of others despite his own condition.

Back to the envelopes. I call George, bring him into a small, dirty interview room and ask him to sit on the stained chair beside the broken table. I sit on the other stained chair. His face is dark and sad. Listless eyes flicker to the ground, hands droop, head and shoulders slump. He is wearing old jeans, well-worn runners and a Liverpool football shirt.

'Did you see the first leg game last night?' I start.

He sniffles and shrugs, 'yeah.'

'Great result', I offer.

Silence. 'How is everything?' I ask and wait.

There's a little rush of speech. 'I can't face it, I can't go on, I've been here before and there's nothing I can do. It never goes away, it's like an animal, got its teeth right in there. And it hurts.'

'I'm sorry to hear this.' I pause. 'But I'm glad you've come here. You have already done something.' Long pause. 'When did this start?'

'Been following me all my life. I'm falling back down the hole since morning. It's bad this time. I'm worried I'll kill myself. I want to step in front of a bus.' He looks at me.

I want to ask how the bus driver's life might change but I don't. I need to assess danger to himself or others. And I need to listen to his story, whatever story he has to tell. He tells me of two previous suicide attempts by overdose. He had drunk seven pints during the match last night. This has undoubtedly increased his fear and anxiety today. I listen to the heart and lungs, looking at arms and legs when checking pulses for any signs of self-harm. I ask him if he has any plans to hurt himself. He says no but I am not so sure. I scan the room for sharp objects before leaving to call psychiatry. Last week a guy poked his head out of a resus cubicle, took a razor from an ECG trolley normally intended to shave a hairy chest and slashed neat lines all down his legs.

'Call Anika', says Ollie, back in the safe haven of the nurse's station after a short debrief. 'She tries to come quickly. Last month, someone left before being seen and drowned themselves in the Liffey.'

* * *

There's a guy with a rash on his abdomen, chest and back. 'When did you first notice this?' I ask.

'A couple of years ago.'

I stare at him.

'My GP referred me to a dermatologist but that appointment isn't for two months so I thought it would be quicker to come here.'

He is a quick discharge, script for anti-fungal cream in hand. I am amazed at why some people choose to spend ten or more hours in an ED waiting room when they know they do not have an emergency condition, delaying assessment for others with chest pain or suspected stroke.

At least he was a quick turnover when I finally saw him. The single piece of feedback junior doctors get on completion of a rotation is not about competency, not about communication, not about which skills to work on. It is on how many patients you got to see on average per shift. There is an underlying tension from above to increase throughput. People are waiting long times as there are too few medics to meet the demand. We are expected to stretch our bodies across the resource gaps and work faster to make up for the short staffing. I am all for optimising productivity, but I worry the urge to be quicker compromises safety. It certainly creates a stress in my mind to keep pushing on relentlessly, don't take that break, forget the cup of water, run all night, get there, get there.

The ED is not an assembly line. Even though long-term averages may be calculated, each patient is unique, and each doctor has their own style. Pressure is placed on staff to work harder, faster and longer to fill resource gaps, when focus should be on the system design. Reverse the flow of expertise. Rather than filter the patient through a series of medical professionals with increasing experience, allowing their sickness to worsen as time slips by, get an experienced doctor to meet them first, order whatever tests are needed, and make a clear plan for management. Weed out the non-emergencies fast and clear out the waiting room.

* * *

The next patient has waited six hours and complains of chronic sweating feet that his GP has been monitoring. When I look, his feet are dry. I sympathise and discharge him with a clutch of information sheets. Excellent, my numbers will be up tonight.

* * *

Marianne's lab results show no toxic substances. I make straight for the waiting room, but she has left again. There is no sign of her the full length of the street outside. I head back to the nurses' station to phone her. 'We're not running an outreach programme you know, if they're gone, they're gone, move on to the next patient', a consultant's past berating rings in my ear as I dial. No answer. I try again after a few minutes to no avail. Should I keep trying? I would go to the ends of the city to offer her support if helping this woman was my only job. She has full capacity to make her own decisions and the gardaí have been in contact with her. I try again before reluctantly moving on.

* * *

Mark's bloods are perfect. They show no sign of infection or inflammation, normal kidney and liver function and no apparent recent damage to his heart. His X-rays look normal. I drop back in and get a jolt when I see him. He is quiet and ashen. He attempts a smile and says how good the care is. There is some common instinct that tells us in a cursory glance that something does not look right. That is all I have to go on. I am like a man on the street with no medical reason, thinking that someone just looks terrible. His vital signs, exams, bloods, X-rays all whisper what the nurse has suggested, 'get him home.' What am I missing?

I phone the surgical SHO on call. I relate the story and ask her to put her hands on him. She is not impressed with his bloods. 'With normal bloods, I won't see them, we have too much on in theatre.' We all get a precious few wild card plays with every colleague and I use one now. My voice firms up. 'I'd really like you to come down, I'm just not happy with him.' She reluctantly agrees but I know she won't rush. Time seeps on. On a whim I phone the radiologist on call who is at home but get a curt answer. 'There is no f…ing way I will come in to do a CT abdo pelvis on someone with no signs.'

* * *

Back at the waiting room, I notice a young girl curled in her mother's arms, a little boy fighting sleep beside her and a man without a chair watching over them. It's rare to see children in the adult ED. I wonder which parent might be sick.

* * *

I meet Anika and introduce her to George. Before I leave, I ask, 'Hey, are you looking forward to Liverpool's return leg next week?'

He smiles faintly. 'Yeah definitely.' An ember of relief and hope glows in all three of us.

I walk the path of discovery with one unwell person after another, sifting for gems of information in stories, searching for signs in their bodies and waiting endlessly for test results to flicker onto a screen. I diagnose and treat urinary tract infections, pneumonias and broken bones. Many other

presentations need immediate action. I stem the blood flow
from a superficial stab wound and suture the laceration,
order scans and subsequent care for a stroke patient, help
clunk a displaced hip back into place and care for a man
who drank too much in the St Patrick's celebrations and fell
on his head. I listen sadly to the story of a fifty-one-year-old
lifelong smoker with significant weight loss, night sweats
and a chronic cough he cannot shake. His eyes are earnest
and blue. He recounts how his father died of what I suspect
he will die from too within months. He tells me how he
misses his father. He says he is determined to give up the
smokes this time as he is young and doesn't want to go the
same way his father did. My heart is full of non-committal
kindness. I order a chest X-ray and know the hour he waits
for the result will be the last of the life he currently knows.

* * *

Familiar faces fill up the observation area. Heroin users
found unconscious in the street are sleeping on each other's
shoulders. A man in alcohol withdrawal is rocking in his seat.
He may be the strongest among us and needs every support
we can give. He sits in lonely sufferance with his drip and
an occasional benzodiazepine to quell the shakes. Security
guards pace the corridors. Someone is asking for a 'Roche'
or a 'D-five', street names for benzos. Someone argues that
the pink and blue envelopes are not gender inclusive. I start
to feel the effects of pushing the body through the night
without sleep. A riot of adrenalin, exhaustion and confused
senses rages in my head. Words to patients are calm and
collected but sound like they have been spoken down a

dark corridor. Back at the station, I squeeze my eyes shut for a moment's respite and my ears are filled with sounds. Hushed words between a patient and a loved one, steady beeping from monitors, someone calling out for a lost childhood friend, someone groaning, someone snoring.

* * *

The surgical SHO tells me to get the gastro guy home. I thank her and look past the curtain at Mark, who is labouring silently. I notice his blood pressure has dropped slightly, despite fluids. When I ask him how he is feeling, he says, 'Not great pal. Whatever it is though, I can handle it. Thanks for looking in on me.' I see Ted the reg come free and grab him.

'I want to run a case past you.' I give him the history, exam and investigation findings. He starts to get impatient and looks down at his notes for another patient. 'Ted, I'm not happy to let him go home.'

Ted locks eyes on me and he takes a punt on my clinical judgement. 'OK, get the bedside ultrasound. I'll have a quick look and if it's normal, get him home.'

Five minutes later, Ted is slopping cold gel all over Mark's abdomen with the ultrasound probe. He slides and fans the probe and we both watch the screen. Ted's face does not flicker at the large span of darkness we are seeing between landmarks. There is fluid where there should not be, lots of it. It is probably blood. He wipes the probe and sighs, 'get the surgical reg.' I turn on my heel. 'And a bed in resus', he adds.

* * *

I drop into the staff kitchen for a cup of water. Mary is gathering leftover sandwiches from the fridge and balancing a jug of water with paper cups.

'Can I help?' I ask.

'It's for the family.'

'Who?'

'The city is full this St Patrick's holiday, and there isn't a hotel or hostel room left. The homelessness agency normally gets them a place but they can't help them tonight. They can't bring kids to the shelters and there is the risk of drugs there anyway, so it's the street or here. They have come to stay warm.'

I grab a few more sandwiches and head out with Mary.

'He had an honest job until recently. They were evicted as they could not pay the rent, simple as that', Mary confides as we take a back corridor.

Mary has brought the family of four to the 'family room', never so aptly needed. It is a small box with two hard couches, adjacent to resus. It is the room used to break bad news to relatives. The little girl is sleeping in her mother's arms, the boy of about seven is watching everything unfold in quiet seriousness. Will he replay this over and over for all his years? This is how a life is shaped. The parents are silent with desperation. I am crying inside. I am so used to treating the medical needs of each person I meet in the ED. There is nothing medically wrong here. I feel like a silent outrage is being committed in front of my eyes. The mother rocks the girl. She looks up at the man, who is stands watching over them, looking beaten and broken-hearted. She reaches out her hand to his.

'Don't be afraid', she whispers. 'There will be better days.'

I pass through the waiting room, stepping through a maze of trolleys, discarded sheets and mobile drips. It is three in the morning. A tepid, humid air rests on lowered heads. Sweat mingles with the waft from forgotten rubbish bins and drying vomit. A few smokers waiting to be called look at me hopefully through the darkened window from outside, faces pale and drawn. I am tired and push on.

I am delighted with myself when I meet Frank, a tall young man, holding his right side and coughing intermittently as we walk to a cubicle. He describes sudden onset, sharp pain in his upper right back, tight chest and immediate shortness of breath. I complete a thorough history and exam, noting increased heart and respiratory rate and resonant percussion of his right upper back. I explain that we should really wait for the chest X-ray but that my suspicion is of a spontaneous primary pneumothorax, also known as a collapsed lung.

'Ya', quips the dad. 'That's what the ambulance driver said as soon as he clapped eyes on him.'

Less delighted with myself.

* * *

Back in the refuge of the nurse's station, Ollie and I are typing notes and chatting. Ted is flicking through the category ones to see what's ahead. The phone goes and staff nurse Matt picks up.

'Is he breathing?' Matt's voice is strained. Everyone in the station goes quiet to listen.

'Right, thank you. Eight minutes.'

We look up expectantly knowing we will all be involved some way in what follows.

'Call from ambulance. Gunshot wound to the face.'

We scramble to resus.

Everybody has a role and a sticker to go with it. The aim is to avoid confusion in a proper emergency. We don gowns and gloves, expecting lots of blood. I pat a sticker that reads 'emergency doctor' to the front of my gown. Ollie pats his to his forehead and a ripple of nervous laughter relieves the tension. We do not know what state this person will be in. Will there be major blood loss, hypovolaemic shock, peri-arrest, airway compromise, loss of facial features, bits of brain hanging out? Arrest and drugs trolleys are wheeled into the cubicle.

The double doors at the end of resus burst open. Two blinding beams of light from the ambulance headlamps blaze into the room. Ambulance doors slam. I squint to see a massive man stride into the resus with giant steps. Para-medics are left trailing in his wake on both sides and a garda hurries behind. We are the ones who are shocked. I had expected a man at death's door to be wheeled, prostrate, to the cubicle. This man is grinning wildly. He is holding a bloodied bundle of rags to the side of his face.

'How are ya horse?' he yells through a bloodied mouth. 'Don't feel a thing.'

He tries to jump up on the bed and needs some persuasion to lie back. He is a huge man. His arms are thick, and their heavy hair is matted with dried blood. A tattoo of a Kalashnikov adorns his left forearm, a tricolour the other. A nurse cuts the shirt off him and the garda stretches an arm out over the medics for it and places it in an evidence bag. Paramedics are describing how he had been found on wasteland known for drug-gang-related assassinations and the pain meds they have given. Slowly, we release his grip on the rags at his face. There is a blackened hole in his cheek and a spray of black gunshot residue down his neck. A close-range hit. The name of the game is stabilisation at first and his vital signs are actually in reasonable shape. We appraise the gunshot site, look for an exit wound, find a clean one behind the mandible and look closely for any streams of blood, of which there are none. Two cannulas go in, blood samples come out.

'OK guys, stand down', Ted says with some relief. 'Away to the scan with him.'

The most surreal two minutes of the night so far.

* * *

A bleary-eyed radiologist reg, who was hauled out of bed, drops by to tell us that Mark has a ruptured splenic artery and was running out of time. He has already told the surgical reg who has taken over care and is prepping for immediate theatre.

'He is out of our hands now', says Ted. 'Good call.'

'Thanks to your ultrasound', I add.

I am thankful to Mark. His compassion for others and steadiness in himself is a beacon of light in the muddled chaos of ED.

* * *

My aim is to try to keep people out of hospital if at all possible. Hospital is a dangerous place. It is a hot, crowded, noisy, resource-strapped reservoir of infection, where almost no one would choose to be except when absolutely necessary. It forces sleep deprivation on sick people and demands that they trade privacy and dignity for regular poking and often impatient questioning from inexperienced doctors who have never been formally trained in bedside communication. If I can find any way to protect someone from the risk of serious hospital acquired infection and the mental trauma of a sleepless night on a wobbly chair in a raucous ED I will. I am glad some instinct was triggered to hold on to Mark a little longer. I am humbled by the kindness he showed everyone else while he was bleeding out and his life nearly ebbed away on an overflow trolley. He was calmness in adversity.

* * *

I help place a drain into the chest of the young man with a collapsed lung and shake my head with relief and satisfaction on seeing a repeat chest X-ray and reinflated lung. I share the good news with the young man and his dad and step out of his resus cubicle.

All seems quiet in the adjacent cubicle where the man with the gunshot hole in his face has been resting. The garda is seated with closed eyes on a chair outside. I think I hear a whisper and strain to listen. It is more a whimper.

'I'm sorry, I'm sorry.'

I pull back the curtain a few inches. He is crying. I walk in and he holds out a hand and takes mine.

'Tell her I'm sorry.'

'Tell who?'

'My Mam. I love her but we had an argument. I said bad things and left her hurting. I went out and shot myself. I didn't mean it.'

I squeeze his hand and tell him everything will work out. I don't hurry. The best thing I have to offer this man with the Kalashnikov tattoo and regret for his death wish is a moment of silence while I hold his hand. Then I find Ted, who has been looking after him, and let him know the latest.

* * *

The pains of hunger for sleep and a black nausea are coursing through me. My head feels cavernous and grotty. Push on.

I look for the first time in twelve hours through a tiny window to the world outside. I see a shock of early morning sunshine high up on the red-bricked terrace across the street. Seeing daylight feels like drinking cool water. The day is arriving, and the solace of handover will come soon.

I gather up notes, make some final referral calls and write discharge letters. Ollie looks bleary eyed but smiles. 'Nearly there', he says quietly. A gentleness seems to overtake us in the final stretch. It has been a shift of pumping adrenaline and intensity under a cover of patient-facing calmness. Now our work is done. There are no fewer patients in the waiting room than when we started out. Their arrival is steady and relentless. We will pass the baton and slip away unnoticed.

I run into Anika, and she tells me she has discharged George. He has agreed to talk therapy and has a first appointment.

'By the way', I say. 'There's a young lady who suffered a terrible ordeal today but self-discharged before getting full care. Do you think you can reach out to her?'

'Leave it with me, of course I will.'

I feel a guilty absolution.

'Thank you', I say. 'Thank you for everything.' Both of us are tired and emotions feel a little loose.

The bright-eyed day team arrive. There is little to handover, and we are gone.

I feel lighter. I wash, throw on a clean t-shirt and head out into the crisp morning air. My eyes hurt and body aches and it feels good. Where has the world been while I was shut away all night? Everything looks new. Where the hell have I been? Did I really see those people? What will become of them? It all feels so distant now, like a dream seeping away into the night that has dissolved.

Cool air flows over me as my bike sails down O'Connell Street and weaves around the street cleaners picking up tattered green paraphernalia. I feel unsteady but happy that I have worked hard. I glance at the Liffey. Its flow is constant like patients though the doors of the ED. I peddle over the waters and my mind is lost in ragged tiredness and thoughts.

This river, this timeless, relentless cascade of energy and life yearning for something greater in the open arms of the sea. It will never stop. Here is permanence, here is proof of life and the enduring spirit of nature. An unbridled torrent of power tumbling along, knowing that things always move on despite our transient human ailments and the fleeting aids with which we shore them up. I love this city, I think again, as the wind slaps me awake, and I love this life. And I cannot wait to sleep.

10.

I WENT OUT FOR A NEWSPAPER

'I hope the author of *Gulliver's Travels*, who left all his wealth to build this psychiatric hospital two hundred and seventy-five years ago, would be happy with what we've done with the place.'

The director's eyes have the pensive wisdom of someone who has been here for half that time.

'We have modernised but held on to the founding values of liberty and human rights. Now, always remain between the patient and the door. If you ever feel your safety is at risk, just press your personal panic button and a trained defence team will descend.'

The director continues his first day welcome talk to new doctors with a list of rules and regulations. My mind drifts and eyes flicker to the windows of the boardroom. The old glass is full of inconsistencies, fired and hardened in an ancient furnace. They make the bright world outside wallow and sway. The arms of majestic chestnut trees that line the hospital avenue dip in the winter wind. They are leaden grey. Knotted fists are clenched at the end of each bare arm, sealed like tombs.

The director is wrapping up, lamenting the few that are lost among the thousands who walk out of here each year lighter and brighter, leaving their shackles behind. He smiles and wishes us enjoyment and good learning. Then with a swirl of his scarf, his introduction is over, and he is gone.

A man with a mop of blonde hair and smile puts his head around the boardroom door. 'I'm Philip, a specialist registrar. If you follow me, we can start the tour.'

I am astounded at the large Mainie Jellett painting hanging in the entrance hall. It is three times the size of the priceless ones hanging in the Hugh Lane Gallery. There is striking art on the walls of every room and corridor.

We are whisked through wards for young and young at heart. We pass through the lockdown ward for those in need of twenty-four-hour support. A new registrar whispers that this is where a medical student had her head shaved on her first day in order to free her from a patient who entangled his fingers in her hair and would not respond to normal defence techniques from the team that descended.

Past the child and adolescent wing, out across the gardens to the addiction services ward. Everything is pristine. Back to the canteen, where Philip explains that lunch money is credited to our staff cards every day. The wonders of working in a private, not-for-profit hospital.

I grab a quick lunch with the other new registrars. The chat is easy and relaxed. We splinter and head to meet the consultants with whom we will be working. Dr Ryan peers over his glasses, smiles kindly and tells me with a soothing

voice that I am just in time for the ward round. Something
in the way he talks tells me that he cares deeply for his
patients, who are all over sixty-five.

In every other discipline, the team goes to the patient.
Here, the 'service user' comes to the team. Eight of us sit
around a business-like table: three psychiatry doctors, a
psychologist, an occupational therapist, a social worker and
two nurses. Service users sit quietly in a line outside, like they
are waiting to be called into the principal's office. Some wring
hands, some clutch scraps of paper with the things they want
to say. It has to be hugely intimidating for anyone coming
through the door to sit in the lonely chair at the top of the
table. In fact, new service users do look stunned at the motley
array of us facing them. Some joke nervously about a firing
squad or a job interview panel. We greet them with friendly
hellos in a vain attempt to soften the stiff, nerve-wracking
formality of what should be a therapeutic interaction. We
tap at our little laptops, demoting eye contact to a cursory
rarity. One of the doctors weaves though a conversation that
explores any progress, examines mental state, uncovers side
effects to medications, occasionally asks openly if they feel
life is not worth living, describes medication adjustments and
finally thanks them for their time. It is like using a hammer
and a six-inch nail to finesse a delicate sculpture. And yet,
even with this brutal tool, the stories weep from stony faces.

* * *

David's glare and tone are fixed as he explains how he sold
his farm at a steep discount to unscrupulous buyers in order
to clear his son's gambling debt.

'I had to help him, he is my only son, my pride and love', his eyes welling. 'But in an instant, I lost everything I knew from my life. The folds of land I knew like the lines in my hand, my daily routine, the work I lived for, my animals, the only real thing I could pass on to my children when I die, my legacy. And every night I wake in a sweat at the price, the price, the price. They snatched it for less than it is worth. And only myself to blame, I signed my life away. Now I am lost in despair.'

We chat through David's progress with him and the various ways our team can offer help. This is the saving grace of the army of professionals in the room. We each have something to offer and can do it in a cohesive way. When David is gone, we chat through what we have learnt and further ideas for supporting him. Dr Ryan rises and pauses before heading through the door to call the next service user. He adds a final reflection, which I realise is a habitual conclusion to every consultation.

'Remember who you are – this is so much greater than what you do.'

He looks away to a distant clock tower through the window. 'And never liquidate your assets for your children before your final shuffle. I'm sad to say that your stock will go down in their eyes, no matter how much they love you.'

* * *

Mary sinks slowly into the chair and releases her grip on the walking frame. Her beautiful blue eyes drift from one of us to the next. 'I'm glad to have come here and met you all. But I don't think there is anything else you can do to help me.

The sadness for my husband and son is too heavy. The little pills and pep talks you give me are bouncing off the thick hide of it. My head is as smashed as the car they were in, and the images haunt me over and over every day. I want to go home.' Dr Ryan chats through her recent falls at home and the need for two people to assist her with mobility. The social worker says she is sure a place will become available at a nursing home within weeks. Mary smiles patiently.

'I want to be among their things. I'm not long for this road. I won't hasten the journey if you worry about that, but I want to be at home for whatever time I have left. My daughters will help me.'

She agrees to sleep on it, and we agree to help her in any way she wishes.

Dr Ryan pauses at the door, 'you never know what is round the corner. Solomon said, "drink your wine with a merry heart."' He eyes the treats brought by the team to get us through the day, 'or in our case, eat the chocolate when it's offered.'

* * *

Joan laughs and proclaims what a stunning day it is. The words tumble out.

'I'm fine I tell ya. I feel as good as the time that I went out for a newspaper and came back with a new sports car instead. The energy at eighty-six is as good as when I was twenty. I could swim an ocean. Sure, I had a dream last night about an old boyfriend', she winks. 'I'd call him today if he was still alive.'

Dr Ryan is lowering her medications online between nods to help attenuate her soaring mood.

'*I went out for a newspaper and came back with a sports car*', he smiles benignly after she has left. 'That would make a great title for a book.'

* * *

Joe unfurls his handwritten note.

'I've been thinking about the time I sold a car to someone thirty years ago. I did not tell him that the wing mirror was loose. I feel terrible about it. I feel like I sold him a pig in a whatsit. I wake every night and can't stop thinking about the crook that I am. And it gets me down you know, fierce low. It was an awful thing to do, wasn't it? And there were times I left work a little early, you know, a few minutes to beat the traffic home, but sure that's just like stealing from the company, isn't it? I'm a cheat and a crook. I should pay some salary back, shouldn't I?'

There are more painful ruminations.

'These thoughts are like thieves', Dr Ryan says. 'When they knock on your door, don't let them in. Why would you let them run amok in your house?'

Joe returns to the office door three times with further questions. Dr Ryan treads a line between counselling and not feeding an insatiable hunger for reassurance. He turns to us when he is gone and says, 'You may wonder about the condition. Labels are not always productive. Focusing on what we can do to help is.'

* * *

Bill is controlled and matter of fact. He rubs his silver stubble.

'Well, I just feel that I am ready to go. In fact, I must go. I don't want to become dependent you know. The mood was savage low certainly and I couldn't get out of bed but now I must. Yes, yes, Annie will be there. I have plenty to keep me busy.'

His answers consist of 'yes', 'no' or 'fine' and shed almost no light on his progress.

I scroll through the history and collateral in the notes to try to understand more. I read that his partner, Annie, lives a completely separate life to him under the same roof. He is terrified of losing his home if he acknowledges the separation, so he carries on as if nothing has changed. He has never once mentioned the separation to anyone. He has also recently retired and cannot adjust to the empty days.

Dr Ryan says he will keep his bed for some days if he changes his mind.

'A trial then, yes a trial.'

Dr Ryan muses after Bill has left, 'flexibility is the single most important trait for lifelong mental health. Roll with the changing world or it will break you.'

* * *

The earnest, decent, open faces keep coming. The ordinariness of the human stories is so clear.

A captain of international industry who is too fond of the drink and struggles to find words; an artist whose children no longer speak to her and describes a suffocating grief; a politician whose mood swings lower and higher than the average person; a global rockstar who carries the weight of the world on their shoulders. Some are a little sicker, believing that their phones are tapped, and news readers are broadcasting secret messages meant only for them.

Every single one is here to get better and rejoin the flow of life. All but Frank, I worry. Frank rests his weary face in his hands during his consultation. He says nothing. Dr Ryan asks kindly how he has been. Frank remains silent. The nurse describes restless nights with broken sleep, poor appetite and asking to be left alone. He returns to the ward, his loose clothes flowing around a thinning and broken man. Dr Ryan adjusts his medications and shakes his head quietly. He has no words of wisdom.

'Please look in on Frank every day', he asks me softly.

* * *

I am tired but inspired by the end of the day. I wander slowly to my bike on the avenue and look up at the barren trees. A train of thought hauls me through a ravaged past as I breathe the icy night air. The greatest voice of hope is the pillaged tree. The remnants of last season's sap are like a dwindling lifeblood. It hungers for the lost love of the sun that once was the heat of life. But even now, deep beneath the silent bark, a new and rising life, yearning to breathe, bursting to explode and taste the sweetness of the world, is gathering strength and swelling in hope that here, in the warmth of fresh sun, eyes and arms and heart will quietly open and bask in heat again. I inhale deeply and start pedalling.

Every day I cycle through the Dublin Liberties to get to work. My eyes are fixed on the tail ends of fuming cars and cracks in the road but my mind wanders to epic events in this iconic quarter. They flash by me. Where flaming whiskey flowed through the streets following an explosion at a distillery and men burned as they gathered it in their hats. Where two young women and their newborn babies perished in the snow as they made their way to a distant hospital many years ago, leading to a new maternity hospital being built at that spot. Where Robert Emmet met his end the day after he declared 'when my country takes its place among the nations of the earth, then and not till then let my epitaph be written' – words that would drive revolutions and which Abraham Lincoln learnt by heart.

There is layer after layer of history, too thick and full to peel.

Heroin addicts clamber up the steps of churches to shelter and sleep in the porches. Tourists and worshipers weave around them to enter the hush of their sanctuaries. Young men argue outside a bookie shop, cigarettes flickering in their bickering mouths. Innovators stroll to the Digital Hub with distracted, dreaming eyes. Artists saunter to the Harry Clarke Building with a hunger. Street sellers cry out. Seagulls wheel and users deal.

Flying past streets with names that evoke the ages. Fishmonger Street, Winetavern Street, Swift's Alley, Lamb Alley, Thomas Street, St James's Gate. Past the countless pubs and dusty shop fronts, the soot clad churches and red brick town houses, the Guinness arch and the art deco whiskey distilleries. Breathing fast and hard. Smells of fresh bread and fish, smoke and roasting hops.

Every day I am humbled and spurred by the depth and colour of life in the city and feel excited for its future. Day after day, I chat with people in the hospital that have made this city or country what it is. Working and shaping the place where we live. I listen and counsel and learn. It seems all of us are born innocent of life's hurt, once lost in play and the endless imagination of childhood, loving our families with wondrous eyes, growing as best we could in the rush of the world about us. Some are caught by an eddy, pulled under by a swirling turbulence or thrust violently against an unforgiving rock, bruised in the maelstrom and tumult of growth. The traumas of childhood leave the deepest scars.

At times I despair at the slow pace of repair. I listen to a lonely cry that they might never get better, the lament that drugs are making them feel washed out. Then there comes a glimmer, a little brightness, a lighter movement, a shy smile at a cast of humour. Best of all, words that grace the healing lips: 'I think I have turned a corner.' I look a little closer and yes, there beyond the veil of the eyes glows a tiny ember in the ashen bed of depression. The first time I hear these words from a woman I have worked daily with for months, I smile to suppress tears, filled by a privilege beyond words. It is a shared, wordless moment. It is a declaration that she is beating her illness. Providence now holds her hand as she walks out of the valley. Our service users fight every day to heal and mostly they do. They walk out lighter and restart their normal lives. They are no different to a person who has passed a painful kidney stone, been given a heart stent or had a hip replaced.

I feel a surge of joy as I leave the hospital one evening and notice the chestnut trees have burst to life. The knotted fists have unclenched. Green open palms have unfurled in the April warmth. The leaves are pulsing with the sap of life, delicate enough for the sun to shine through them, revealing an intricate network of veins.

Then I do my first night shift.

'You'll get some sleep', they said. 'It's way easier than paediatrics call', they said. It probably is. But I never heard such stories when I was called to a distressed service user in the black of night.

'I flew off the mountain, they stretchered me back, I went to Indonesia and stayed warm with sticky tape, look, nothing, I have written it down, these signs are an affront to my rights, I trust you because I can see your aura but I won't take those meds, and I can sense the evil spirits in the light bulb, the devil is waiting.' Manic words in a pressure of speech from a man whose family describe him as kind and loving and who has spent his life caring for older people with terminal conditions.

I am called to the addiction ward. A woman I meet there laughs and says, 'I'm so glad I was sick yesterday.'

'Why is that?'

'Cause Bernie, Dec and Milly climbed over the wall last night. They crossed the river to the hotel, and texted the lot of us that the party was in room 323. It woulda been mental. They are absolutely wasted now. All that work to get off the gear and they are back in the deep end tonight, probably sleeping rough again. I'm glad I was sick yesterday, cause you know what, if I was well enough I woulda gone with them.'

I eye the fifteen-foot wall as I walk across the yard to the nurse's station, wondering how they managed to break out. The nurses are replaying CCTV of a different incident.

'There, right there, look', one says.

I peer over their shoulders and see grainy, black and white footage of a young man crossing the yard earlier in the evening. Something falls from his pocket.

'What is it?' I ask.

'See for yourself, Mary found it by luck on the path earlier.' They motion to a bag of white powder on a desk.

'You're kidding me', I gasp.

'Gardaí are on their way to pick it up and take the video tape. That fella who was in here for drug rehab was thrown out last week after he was seen snorting coke off the breakfast table. Now he is back dealing to the people he met when he was in. Wrecking the lives of other people who are trying to get better.'

I visit the service user I have been called to see. He is a young schoolteacher with a three-thousand-euro-a-week cocaine habit.

'Is there something you can give me, something that can help the anxiety? It is fierce tonight. I feel awful low, and I won't be able to sleep', he says gently with pleading eyes. Drug-seeking behaviour is gentle and kind, like a whispering breeze seeking a crack through which to seep. I reach for ways to stem the craving that does not involve chemicals which could create further dependency. I ask him to tell me his story.

He explains tearfully how someone brought coke to a weekend teacher party. The high was one hundred times more intense than his greatest ever pleasure. Something in his genes was unleashed. He has chased that first high ever since. He could not stop, and it came at a cost. He lost his job, his partner and his home. He crawled the streets looking for targets, an easy handbag, a mobile phone snatch, anything that could feed the screaming need. His dealer let his debt soar to over fifty grand. One night he was cornered by the dealer and two associates. The dealer took his hand, placed a gun in his palm and gave him a name. Kill this man and clear your debt or be killed in one week he was told. That was last week. I stare in silence at his gaunt face. A certain resolve has crept back into his eyes.

'Me ma is going to sell her house to clear my debt. I'm going to get clean in here, then get a job and pay her back.'

We agree that dependency-forming anti-anxiety medicine is best avoided tonight.

I pass by Frank's room back in the main hospital. The door is ajar. I stop and listen as if for my own child's breath. Good, he is asleep. I have called to him daily. Our chats have mainly been one-way. He nods occasionally and I keep things short to respect his space. I have yet to see any improvement in his mental state.

There are calls through the early night from people in the community, saying they are suicidal. It is so hard to know what the right thing to say is. Mostly, I listen to their stories. I wonder if they are sitting in a dark kitchen or on the edge of a bed. I gently probe for real intent or planning and encourage them to come to the hospital, attend their local emergency department or seek out a loved one's company. I am wracked with helplessness at the distant end of a phone line. We make a plan for the hours ahead and people very often say they feel better after the chat. A problem shared.

I retreat to my room. There are three rings of protection for the service users. Firstly, the wards are locked. Secondly, the building is locked. Thirdly, the high walls and gates are closed to the world outside. I lay my head down in a little room off a dark corridor between the first and second rings. Sleep comes slowly.

I am jolted awake at one a.m. by the medical emergency bleep. I dart down the corridor, tucking in my shirt, and arrive at a ward to help stem the blood from the back of a man's head. He has fainted, struck his head and lacerated the occipital area. He is oriented, pupils are equal and reactive to light and a basic neurological exam uncovers no abnormalities. As I suture, he recounts nightmares about violent abuse he received in school many years ago that woke him in a nauseous frenzy. He had jumped out of bed, was overcome with dizziness and doesn't remember hitting the ground. I decide against a transfer for a CT scan of the brain and cannot sleep subsequently as I replay that decision.

An hour later, I am attending an eighty-year-old woman. She describes indigestion that she often experiences and asks for an anti-acid remedy that her GP has been prescribing for this. She says the pain has gone completely within minutes. I listen as a nurse tells me he is convinced the pain was associated with her generalised anxiety. I ask for an ECG when he can complete one. He calls me back to review the ECG and I finish some paperwork I had started before returning. I expect to see nothing abnormal and have a pen raised to sign it, then stop dead. I ask the woman how she feels, and she says the pain has come back but it is very slight and under her right breast, less typical for heart pain. She is pacing the room, chatty, and complains about the noise from other service users on the ward. She is annoyed to hear that it is worth doing some additional tests. There is a muted conversation over my shoulder about the difficulty of ordering bloods in this hospital in the night. I turn to the night staff and say she needs to go to the emergency department right now in an ambulance with three hundred milligrams of aspirin under her tongue. I kick myself that I did not see her sooner. I kick myself that I did not stay for the ECG. Time is muscle. She has three stents placed within an hour to help abate an advanced heart attack. I was thrown by the woman's vigour and description of recurrent indigestion, by the nurse's conviction about anxiety, by the atypical, disappearing pain and the lack of other usual symptoms. Next time I will place the ECG leads and read the heart's electricity before the paper has finished printing.

I get a call to review a service user's bleeding hand.

'What happened?' I ask the nurse.

'He punched the suggestion box and shouted, "that's what I think of this f…king place."'

The night gives way to light, and I work through the next day to plug a resource gap, stretching my shift to 36 hours. Work might be an overstatement as I am not much good for anything. I sit with a psychologist friend for lunch. He is not a fan of the gloopy soup du jour. He does not want to waste it by throwing it out. He shrugs and says with a smile he now has four choices. He can change the soup (by lashing in a heap of chilli); he can change how he feels about the soup (by convincing himself it is full of good stuff and will serve to get him through the day); he can manage discomfort (by distracting himself in our chats while gulping it down); or lastly, he can be unhappy. That's three good choices for any problem that life presents.

I am bleeped by admissions to assess two unplanned presentations. The first is a Mr Murphy. I head to the admissions lounge and stretch out a hand to the tired-looking man pacing there.

'Mr Murphy?' I ask. He nods and launches into a whispering monologue in the third person.

'He hasn't slept in two days, you know. He hopes there will be a quiet place here, a place to rest and heal.'

I bring him to one of the assessment rooms and since he sits on the edge of the bed rather than the chair, I decide to start with taking his vital signs. My mind is clocking through the possible differentials as his words tumble out in a rush. I have his jacket sleeve off and blood pressure cuff wrapped around his arm when he stops suddenly.

'No, it's me brother. Me brother is the one to be admitted.'

We both laugh with embarrassment, and I lead him back to the lounge and find his brother in a different room with a nurse.

The second presentation is a man in his thirties sitting in his sister's car in the car park, refusing to come into the building. His sister has driven him here as she is at her wits end trying to care for him. She meets me at the entrance and says he is psychotic and has been aggressive at home, smashing furniture and pushing her around. She says he had been admitted here previously for treatment of cannabis addiction, but his use had triggered an unrelenting psychotic state. We explain that we can only assess and consider admission if he joins us voluntarily. She asks me to talk to him at the car and I go out with a nurse to see how we can help. I try to chat with him at the passenger door. He is a big man. He glares straight ahead, rolling a cigarette, then smokes it fiercely in three drags. The sister suggests she call her other brothers to come down and 'convince' him to go in. We chat through a little further the idea of a voluntary admission. She cries and says no one will help her. The man gets out of the car and towers above me well within a space that would be comfortable. He glowers wordlessly. It takes a lot to intimidate me, but his intensity is fearful. The mobile panic button is out of signal range in this sprawling car park. I offer to give them space to think about things and that we are here for him if he should wish to come inside. I shudder when I close the door of the doctor's office. I open his previous notes on my laptop to add an update. I read through how he had last been discharged for drug use in the hospital, intimidating other service users and threatening to murder every staff member who had worked with him, calling out their names as he left the building. The clinical director has barred him from any readmission. I am only a little ashamed when I scrawl my signature illegibly on the referral letter to the local emergency department, which I feel is the best alternative. Still, I think about how he got out of the car when he saw his sister upset and wonder how the right approach might tap into the man who instinctively cares for his family and find a way back home from his so-called 'soft drug'-induced hell.

The clock's arms swing slowly towards the day's end, and I am dying to sleep. Dr Ryan calls and asks if I wouldn't mind doing his weekly talk to all the assembled over seventy-five-year-old service users in the hospital as he has been called to an emergency. I have no choice. I go for gloopy soup option two and embrace that it will be good for me.

'Oh, by the way, the talk is in fifteen minutes. Sorry, I owe you one.'

I have no time to prepare so I turn to something I know well and jot down four questions on a torn sliver of an envelope, not even the full back of it. I grab a couple of cartons of milk from the fridge on the way to the education room.

'Would anybody here be interested in weightlifting?'

Faces that wear the years of experience look at me as if I am mad. They shift their sticks and walking frames and wait. Not one hand.

We talk about bodybuilders and laugh a little about the *Terminator* movies. I am surprised when Frank, who has been wrestling his demons and not spoken in days, whispers that he used to lift weights as a young man. There is a glow of warmth from others in the room on hearing his voice. We breathe in the kindness of the group.

'What does frailty mean to you?'

There is a wistful discussion about growing old, losing the strength of youth and the constant fear of falling. I share the thought of a frail tree falling easily in the wind, weave in medical definitions, describe how frailty is a state of vulnerability, and share the fact that everyone starts to lose muscle and bone mass from their thirties.

'Becoming frail is a one-way street as you get older, isn't it?' offers a man.

'And once you're frail, there's no going back', offers another.

'There is a natural transition between frailty and resilience', I say. 'We are all on that path as sure as we are human beings, young and old. So, the truth is that we are all frail. Equally though, the truth is we are all resilient.'

I pause and watch the doubtful faces.

'What if frailty could be delayed and even reversed? What if simple activities could stop our march towards what most people believe is inevitable and irreversible. What if we could turn that transition around and stride instead towards resilience, improving our health, avoiding illnesses, falls, dependency and even early death? I have spent years researching everything ever published about interventions for frailty. It is possible to delay it. It is possible to reverse it.'

'How might we do that?' Joan asked the last of the four questions I had jotted down.

My eyes flicker to Frank. He raises his head slowly with a faint, forgotten smile.

'By lifting weights', he says.

'Yes', I nod gratefully. 'Not in the way the media and movies portray. In a simple, everyday way we can do in the comfort of our own homes.'

I grab the couple of two-litre cartons of milk by their handles and go through a few easy exercises in my chair that bear weight on all the upper body muscle groups. I show a few more exercises for legs that can be done while standing and holding the back of a chair.

'Only four percent of over sixty-five-year-old people who did these exercises for twenty minutes, four times a week, progressed to frailty after a year in a study by a colleague, Mateu Serra-Prat. Four times as many who did not do the exercises went from being robust to being frail in a year. And by the way, drink the milk afterwards as an easy means to get the protein building blocks for strength.'

I ask my first question again. All the hands go in the air with a few laughs.

'Sorry I don't have a sheet with those exercises to give you. It is something I must make.'

The day is over at last. I have seen so much complexity and suffering in the last 36 hours, and I do not know if I have helped much. As I drag my feet past reception on the way home, I look at the Mainie Jellett painting, as if to let the abstract strokes transport my mind away from the raw reality of life within these walls. I see it as a work of pure beauty. I peer a little closer and notice the canvas is becoming unstuck at the edges and has been lathered with cheap glue. I sigh, deflated. It is a fake. Is that what we do here? Are we pretending that a dollop of chemical will stick life back together in a frame of encouraging words? How much of what we offer really works? How much is a placebo? Does it really matter?

I saunter over the granite threshold worn smooth by thousands before me and through the massive oak doors. The leaves on the majestic chestnut trees look wan and tired. They droop, dusted and drunk with life and the dewy ether of roasting hops and industrial alcohol from nearby distilleries.

I hear my name being called. I turn and there is Frank.

'I was thinking', he said. 'You told us you'd make a leaflet with those exercises so people can do them when they go home. Use me. Photograph me doing the exercises. I don't have much to give but I spent a life learning how to be fit. That black dog wrestled me to the ground soon after I gave up exercising. I know now how important it is to stay as physically strong as possible. Resilient like you said.'

I stare half-exhausted and feel so grateful. Not only for his idea but for the fact that a man who craved privacy and stayed locked in his room for weeks, saying nothing, was offering help and creating this legacy for himself and others.

We agree to work on the photos in the coming days and clasp hands. He pauses before walking back in and says, 'You know, I think I have turned a corner.'

I watch him walk away, then fill my lungs and pedal home through the distiller's mist.

11.

THERE IS NO CURE FOR HOPE

*T*he text messages start early in the morning.

'I've never seen anything like it, I can't get out of the house.'

'Can anyone make it in?'

'They need the drugs.'

'They need the chats.'

I throw open the bedroom curtains and I'm dazzled by snow falling thickly, softening the world.

'I can do it.' I want to do it. I am loving working at the hospital for older people.

Three beautiful girls watch from the window as I stumble though a three-foot pile of snow on our garden path. I look over my shoulder at a scene like a Christmas card. A patient, loving Mum cradles our daughters, happy and waving, in each arm. I've promised snow fun in the park to the big little one when I get back. I swing my arms and pretend to slip and fall, sending them into a fit of giggles. Then I turn and launch into the untouched snow.

The air is dripping with an orange light of sunrise, and it glows on the snow drifts. There is peace where cars and commuters normally rumble. I stop crunching in my hiking boots on Ranelagh main street and listen to the dawn unravelling. Nature has taken back this city with a sweep of snow.

On a tree above, a solitary leaf clings to its branch. It has seen the winter through. A whisper of wind passes, and the leaf gives up its lifelong grip. Perhaps the last moment of a life is its greatest. Spinning, sparkling, turning over and over. A golden dancer with russet and wine, sailing through the morning sunshine. It is finally free from the tree that gave it life. This moment alone marks its uniqueness. It is the centre of its universe and sails with the breeze. Its descent is glorious. Never before has it moved so gracefully, so far and so free. It never will again. The fall is complete. When it settles to the earth, it is for eternity. There it will rest, soften, retreat into soil, ferment, content to offer its goodness to nature's cycle. Life is over, and begins again.

I pass through the secret side gate, across the breathtaking expanse of white where cars normally park and under the pillared portico to the gush of heat in the entrance hall. This hospital supports older people recovering from surgery, stroke or trauma. I peel the Everest gear off me, dump it in the doctors' office and head to the wards.

Some night shift nurses have agreed to stay on to cover colleagues who are stranded at home by snow. They are bright with chats. The clinical nurse manager has cracked open a tin of chocolates that was being saved for a special occasion.

'What can I do to help?', I ask.

We go through the jobs and divide them up. One of my colleagues, Jack, has texted to say he will also trek in, and we leave jobs on Willow Ward for him.

I work from person to person. A sore ankle, a swollen hand, difficulty sleeping, a medication adjustment, a respiratory exam, a long listen to a rumination. It is all straightforward thankfully. The morning is full of conversation, reassurance and a watchful eye for anything that might kick off later in the day, such as a cough that might burrow deeper and trigger delirium or a low-grade temperature that might quickly progress to sepsis. I hope no one will need a transfer to the general hospital for acute care as road crews have yet to clear tons of snow blocking the long drive.

I head to the steaming canteen to tuck into homemade sandwiches and tea. Jack has made it in and is recounting an interaction with a patient to a small group of nurses.

'"Are you serious?" I asked her.'

'"I am", she says.'

'Sure, there's five feet of snow outside.'

'"Sure, I have my stick", she says', and Jack bursts into laughter.

Jack turns to me. 'Mrs Cleary wanted to go home to mind her dogs. Can you believe it? Eighty-nine and thin as a waif.'

'Is someone coming to collect her?' I ask.

'No, that's the whole thing. She lives alone. I asked her how she thought she'd get home. "I'll get the bus", she says. The bus! Firstly, I don't think the buses are running and secondly, she wouldn't make it to the end of the drive before perishing in the snow.'

My back and neck feel hot.

'It gets better', he says. 'She's here for rehab after a hip replacement only four days ago. Can you believe it?'

'They get them walking within a day now', says a nurse.

I'm munching on a sandwich. 'What about her capacity?' asks another.

'Ah capacity, don't talk to me.' His grin fades a little and he looks away. 'Listen, she broke her hip falling off a chair trying to get a hatbox off the top of her wardrobe. I asked her, "now would you do that again, get up on a chair?" "No, I wouldn't", she says and just when I think she has seen sense she adds, "sure, I have the hat now. Not unless I wanted to get something else from on top of the wardrobe." Now you tell me if she has capacity. She has poor mobility, a high risk of falling and little insight into dangers and consequences. There is no one to mind this vulnerable lady, no food in the fridge and a snowstorm raging. What would you do?'

Mrs Cleary's conversation with me on previous days had wandered. She shared stories about how her father fought in wars of the last century. She missed her dogs, a black setter and a Jack Russell, who were being minded by a neighbour. I sensed a clear-minded comfort in herself. But I had not seen her today and I cannot say anything about her current capacity, her ability to understand and retain information, then weigh it up to make and communicate a decision. I was not there for Jack's interaction. I can't say what I would do. Still, something bothers me deeply. Is it the off-hand discussion about her? Is it that lack of clarity on her capacity or a lack of understanding of her wishes? Then it strikes me. This is about autonomy. How brutally easy it is to snuff it out without doing absolutely everything we can to preserve it.

The rest of the lunchtime chats pass by me. I am lost in two imagined evenings unfolding, his and hers.

Jack goes home, whistling to the wind. He throws his bag in a corner with abandon and the feeling that the workday is done and behind him. He lashes a dinner in the microwave and is delighted not to miss the start of a reality TV dating programme he has been glued to every week.

Mary Cleary lies sweating in her bed. There is a riot in her head. A bewildered confusion rages through her. Freedom is gone. It has been ripped from her like a spoon gouging pulp from a fruit. The shell of her mind feels brittle and delicate. Something has changed and is lost forever, like land collapsing into a massive fissure. The ability to choose for herself, in every living moment of adulthood, that has weaved the fabric of who she is, means nothing anymore. Freedom is what people lay down their lives for. This is what her father fought for in France, clutching a rifle and smelling death as he crawled through no-man's land. What would he say now? Where are you Father when I need you to hold me in your arms. Take me out of here Daddy, I want to go home. The weight of this blanket is like lead. She cannot move a finger. She feels trapped and scared, like the child of herself, hiding, shivering, curled up and crying.

Melodramatic? Taking someone's freedom is a massive life event. I think people know enough to feel a sense of being trapped, held hostage by a well-meant word or the cruel needle tip of a cannula, with or without capacity. Autonomy has primacy. It is a societal value that many have died for so that their children may know it freely. But with the stroke of a pen or the tap on a keyboard, it is whipped away unthinkingly from some of the most vulnerable people in society, night after night after night. 'It's what is best for the patient', is the routine, blindly paternalistic salve for the conscience.

Jack and I walk slowly back to the ward.

'Don't take this the wrong way Jack, it just feels wrong to stop someone from going if they express any wish to go. I don't think it's even legal. There was a case of a lady in a nearby hospital who wanted to go home. Staff feared for her safety, believed she lacked capacity and felt it was in her best interests to stay. The family took the hospital to the High Court arguing unlawful detention. When the judge backed the hospital, the family appealed and won. The Court of Appeal ruled that even when someone did not have capacity or staff believed it was in the patient's best interests, the hospital had no right to hold a person. Detention has no place in medical care.'

'But we have a duty of care to our patients. What if leaving the hospital would mean a certain deterioration, or worse, death?'

'Nothing is certain. Look, I understand where you're coming from. But put yourself in her place.'

'What about common law protecting someone making an intervention to save a life, like grabbing a fella before he jumps off a bridge? What about the doctrine of necessity that allows life-saving treatment without consent? What about the Medical Council guide to professional conduct and ethics telling us to decide what is in the patient's best interests if they lack capacity and there's no next-of-kin around or anyone else with legal authority?'

'Yep, there's lots of contradictions', I admit.

'So, unless you want to hold someone under the Mental Health Act or seek a ward of court order, neither of which apply to Mrs Cleary, a person is free to limp out the door to a possible disastrous end. That makes no sense to me. We must do what's best for people under our care and protect them from coming to harm. You know, first do no harm and all that', says Jack.

'All the same, what I like about the appeal judgement is that it comes down on the side of autonomy', I add.

'One of our four old-fashioned pillars of medical ethics', he says.

'Is it better to let a few go home and come to harm than compromise a basic human freedom?' I wonder aloud.

We look quietly at each other, seeing both sides and appreciating the open discussion that has got us here.

Jack pulls out his phone and dials the consultant on call that day. As he chats through the dilemma, he is cut short, and I hear words to the effect that under no circumstances should Mrs Cleary be let home that day.

'Well, I have my orders', sighs Jack.

'He is covering himself', I say and shake my head.

'Is he? Or is he using his common sense and years of experience?'

'He is not here and has not spoken to her. We are here and are well within our rights to make this call.'

'Are you gonna say that to a coroner in court?'

He studied my worried face. Then he smiled. 'Damn it, maybe we'll say it together.'

We pass the lobby and see the snow trucks have cleared a path to the door.

We sit with Mrs Cleary. We chat through the pros and cons of her decision and the hazards of being on her own. It becomes clear she has full capacity. She wants to go home. We smile and nod. Her eyes are clear, crisp blue. They dance.

She takes Jack's hand to thank him.

'Mrs Cleary', he asks. 'Would you allow me to care for you at your home tonight?'

She squeezes his hand.

'I've been doing this a long time, minding myself and my little dogs', she says gently. 'I know my home; I know what I can do and I know my limits. I can do this. If it makes you feel better, you can accompany me and you're welcome to stay. You'll see. We'll be fine.'

He turns to me and says with a resigned smile, 'I'll just think of it as a night shift.'

'And tomorrow night?'

'We can cross that bridge tomorrow. This is what she wants today. Let's pull every favour we have with social services and hope we can get night-time support.'

Mrs Cleary looks through a window at the snow falling again.

'You can fix or medicate many things, like this old hip … but there is no cure for hope', she says.

I produce fifty euro from my pocket and stuff it into Jack's. 'For the taxi.'

* * *

I spend the afternoon in the tiny doctor's office working on a frailty and resilience research paper and minding the pager in case there are calls from the wards. The radiator creaks and groans as it throws off heat and keeps the freeze clawing at the window at bay. I worry about whether we have made the wrong decision. The legal and medical systems and an indignant media could turn on us if she has a bad outcome at home. The consultant will demand an explanation. Nothing would be said if she stayed safe in hospital for a few more nights. Then I realise it was never our decision to make.

I lose myself in the paper I am writing. I have systematically analysed everything ever written and published on interventions to delay or reverse frailty. 'See how the wind overturns the frail tree', Buddha said some two-and-a-half thousand years ago. I think of Mrs Cleary in a gust of wind. I feel everyone has an inherited instinct for recognising frailty. It has only been defined in medical terms in recent years. Only four of the nine hundred and twenty-five academic papers I have analysed were published before the start of the decade. It reflects a shift in medical focus from systems, such as cardiovascular or respiratory, to caring for the whole person. The novelty of focus on frailty as a construct also creates fertile ground for shaping it and how we help people who are frail. I think I have identified a new way to screen for frailty and a new way to compare diverse interventions. I am filled with hope as I learn how frailty is not the one-way street that most people believe but can be reversed with interventions as simple as strengthening exercises and good dietary protein. This is the hope I want to share in the paper. We can reverse one of the greatest scourges of growing older. I hope it will help Mrs Cleary and every single one of us lucky to get to her stage. I grind through the analysis, scribble some charts and tap out the words.

The winter darkness has descended when I look up. I wander out to the quiet nurse's station. The new night team is settling in. Mrs Cleary has gone home. I take a long breath. I have a strong sense that she will be okay. No matter when her last days come, let them be great, let them be of her own choosing. I have a promise to keep, and I trudge away to play in the snow under lamplight.

12.

SPINNING AROUND

'*T*here's a worm at the bottom of the garden and his name is Wiggly Woo.'

I smile when I hear these words. They are sung gently. I can hear the woman's smile in the loving lilt of her voice. I sing them to my own beautiful daughters, and I think of how they laugh at my funny faces when I sing. There is a perfect beat being drummed in rhythm with the song. A dull thrum. What is that sound? I peer around the corner of the room. A mother is looking softly at her child. Her smile is wide, her eyes animated and overflowing with love. She is pounding her child's chest purposefully. A cough, a desperate hack, a long whistling gasp, a deep gurgling release, the whites of the eyes roll, she tries so hard and at last the suffocation loosens and phlegm burbles up. Her mother gathers it with a tissue, leans forward and kisses her beautiful girl on the forehead, then keeps singing in a whisper.

The paediatric consultant raps lightly on the door and we enter the room. Mum looks up, full of hope. The seven-year-old child has never moved or talked since birth. She can breathe and move her eyes. She watches us. The consultant chats with Mum and we review the vital signs together. He places his stethoscope on the girl's chest. He lifts it and replaces it, then lifts and taps it. His brow furrows and eyes widen, then soften and he starts to chuckle. A rasping cackle arises from the girl and her eyes dart with delight.

'Ah, that is so funny, you got me again.'

Mum is grinning. 'Come on darling, let the doctor listen to your lungs properly.' She turns to us. 'She always does this. It is her game, her little joke on us all. She holds her breath when someone tries to listen to her lungs, just to get a reaction.'

She can do little. What she can do is breathe and she uses this to create fun. I want to stop the world and yell that this child is the strongest, most beautiful, smartest kid you could ever meet.

* * *

It seems like countless moments such as this are all I am left with at the end of my paediatric rotation. Flashes that present and retreat into shadow. Month after endless month of sensory jolts, brutal weekly or twice weekly twenty-five-hour shifts, peppered among normal day shifts, fuelled by microwave dinners in a resident room with flickering industrial overhead lights.

I sit now in an outpatient clinic room awaiting a patient on the very last afternoon of my training in this children's hospital. My mind is awash with thoughts of the winter months here. The window is ajar to let some stifling hospital heat escape. Smoke from dressing-gowned patients gathered at the entrance to the adjacent adult hospital drifts back into this asthma clinic.

My mind turns to that res room, sitting quietly at four in the morning and recovering from an intense few hours in the emergency department. I am thinking of another little girl, two years old, the same age as my own daughter. I can see her little chest working hard, heaving and collapsing almost every second. There are troughs in her skin underneath her ribs, a deep dimple beneath her sternum and ridges along her neck as every accessory chest and neck muscle strains to suck in the oxygen her body craves. A machine blows the maximum flow of oxygen through a facemask. Her eyes are closed, her lips are blue. The senior reg is suppressing his panic. The anaesthetics reg he has called whispers into her phone to bring the crash trolley. These are the two most senior people in the hospital at this hour and they have tried everything they know to get this girl's respiratory distress under control. Every appropriate medication has been deployed and breathing supports put in place. The parents linger at the back of the room, unaware that their baby is on the cusp of an arrest. I am holding various needles, nebuliser masks and blood vials, silently deferring to the reg's requests for help. I have already shared every idea I could offer. I feel utterly helpless. Then it happens. It is almost imperceptible. The girl's body relaxes, as if taking a rest from her rapid breathing. This is followed by a violent resumption of her gasping effort to cling to life. She is the embodiment of resilience. Every iota of strength is devoted to her breathing effort, everything else slips from consciousness. At that moment of subtle apnoeic relaxation, a herald of the body giving up, my eyes flicker to the anaesthetics reg. Her tense shoulders melt and what seems to me to be a surge of both resignation and anger clouds her face. She had asked the paeds reg to call the consultant sooner and he had agreed reluctantly. It is too late to transfer to an ICU several miles across town. Whatever is going to happen will unfold within minutes. Respiratory arrest, vital organ and brain damage, cardiac arrest. My head screams and heart bursts as I watch the fight fade in this perfect and innocent child.

There is a change in the air as the consultant sweeps in. She is completely at ease. She asks for the latest details. Her eyes are bright and relaxed, as if teasing out a conundrum. She turns to the senior reg and incredibly makes this a teaching moment. She says he has done everything she would have except for one thing. She tells him he has two levers to pull for the oxygen supplementation, flow and volumetric fraction. The reg kept increasing the oxygen flow in response to the girl's falling oxygen levels but to no effect. She leans over to reduce the flow and adjust the concentration. A screen blinks as the girl's oxygen saturation starts to creep up and her pounding heart rate falls. Soon the girl's breathing soothes towards a regular pace. Her life is saved. The team can stand down.

How could it have come to this? Somewhere in a storm of tightly resourced hospital staff, lack of frontline experience and early morning exhaustion, a little girl stared death in the face. I take five in the res room.

A Canadian reg colleague joins from the ward. She listens as I share what has happened, my words tumbling under the gravity of despair. She is kind and listens with care. Then she takes the opportunity to debrief for the first time how she led chest compressions following the arrest of a little boy weeks previously in another hospital. The cause was lost. The senior reg called it. A nurse whispered to keep the compressions going. 'Why?', they asked. 'Because the parents want to wait until a priest arrives to baptise him.' I am stunned. In the darkened room, both of us sit silently, punch drunk, refusing to let the tears roll because at any moment our bleeps may go and require us to sprint.

I am haunted by the recurring thought that there is nothing more frightening to me than a doctor running in a hospital corridor, when the life of a child might hang in the balance.

I get up from my seat to close the window in my outpatient clinic room and block out the cigarette smoke.

I walk out to the corridor where children and their parents are gathering for other clinics. Some children sit snugly in their mum's or dad's arms, some draw pictures with the crayons and paper laid out, some sit quietly swinging their legs underneath big chairs, watching everything going on around them. Many know this place from their regular visits. They meet generally kind nurses and doctors who do funny tests and ask them and their mums and dads loads of questions. The youngest eyes reflect a sense that anything and everything is possible. Older eyes can be wary with knowledge and the memory of one too many needle sticks.

The first of my patients arrives, a young boy accompanied by his mum. We go through spirometry results and chat about recent symptoms. I listen to his chest. There is quiet in the room. A mild, muffled wheeze transmits from otherwise clear lungs. I ask him to breathe a few more times. My eyes stray to the window as the sound of his firm breathing reminds me of the rhythmic breathing support machines in the high dependency unit.

Every morning over recent months I had stopped by the high dependency unit to check new patient charts and gather data for a research project. I was mapping levels of lactate in the blood after administration of a nebulised medicine. It might be useful for emergency doctors treating children in respiratory distress. I remember the morning I ignored the charts and joined the huddle of doctors peering at an image on a phone. The image showed a large white mass in a young boy's brain. So, this is why he had been convulsed with seizures overnight after a late presentation, this is why the anti-epileptic medicine had no effect. There was little said among the team. I looked through the window at the mum and dad holding a limp hand each. The boy's breaths were steady and calm. He would be transferred to the ICU but to no avail sadly. He was the only patient who did not go home over the four winter months I spent in paediatrics. Every other child I met walked or skipped out the door, by far the best rate compared to any other discipline or age group I have worked with.

I snap back to the present.

'How old are you now?', I ask the boy as I look in one ear.

'Six and a ha', he says.

'Six and a half? You are getting so tall.'

'No', he says earnestly. 'Six and a ha. I was just six and I am not yet six and a half.'

I ask him to spin around. He twirls around several times until his mum explains I just want to look in the other ear. He sees the funny side and laughs. There is every chance that his symptoms will resolve completely with time, as his two older siblings have experienced. We go through inhaler technique again and adjust his maintenance medication before they leave for what they say is a customary treat in a local café. Mum's eyes crinkle as she says she hardly gets one-on-one time with her son and treasures these six-monthly appointments. Sometimes our health forces us to step away from the tumult and breathe, simply breathe.

I am bleeped to drop back up to the ward briefly. A four-year-old boy being treated for a respiratory infection and dehydration has lodged something up his nose and I am asked to try to help get it out. It is a delicate act as the boy cradles in his mum's arms. Her arm is deftly wrapped around both of his to keep him relaxed and stop him swatting me. After painstaking manoeuvres, I have a grasp on the foreign body with long tweezers, which turns out to be a jellybean. Just as I am bringing it into the light of day again, I ask him why he put it in his nose. His mum sees the jellybean emerging and releases her hands to clap with relief. He grabs it with a free hand and shoves it deeply into his other nostril. I have rarely seen such dexterity. Then he winks, for which skill at such a young age I feel admiration, and says nasally, 'I wanted to feed my brain.'

* * *

There are cracks in time while waiting. Waiting for a patient. Waiting for results. Waiting for a consultant to arrive for handover or a ward round. I fill these up with research. Sometimes curiosities arise. Why things are the way they are and what would happen if we tried to improve them. I feel compelled to find answers, jot them down and share them in publications. I design new interventions, mine data or tap away at a paper while waiting instead of punching a button on the snack machine or flicking though my phone. Some of this has been fruitful. I recall the jolt of enjoyment on learning that my systematic review on interventions to delay or reverse frailty had been accepted for publication. Two long years of rigorous research in tandem with my clinical work was finding the light at last. The journal took the opportunity to do a press release on the day of publication. During a December night shift after a full day, I finished a ward round and stole a moment to search for its initial impact. I had not looked all day but close to three a.m. I succumbed to vanity and did a quick online search. I was shocked. It had been published as a mainstream news story on the front page of Irish and UK broadsheets, no doubt promoted to fish-and-chip wrap at that very hour. It had featured as news throughout Europe, the US and Australia. It had been discussed and analysed on international TV and radio shows. It had gone viral on multiple international lifestyle sites. The message of hope that frailty is not an inevitable one-way street but can be delayed and even reversed seemed to have caught a wave of interest. The interventions that proved most effective and easiest to do were straightforward resistance training and appropriate dietary protein. The simplicity of this approach was compelling, and the paper would go on to be the most read in the journal during that year, one of the most cited in its history, and become the start of a research journey in frailty and resilience. My ego was duly buoyed and then dumped as I flitted to a line under the photo of an aging citizen munching on an overflowing sandwich: 'Elderly Brits can slash risk of falling by regularly eating tuna mayo sandwiches', a notorious tabloid boasted. Several years' toil, studious attention to detail and finessed conclusions had found their way to this attention-grabbing headline that strayed liberally from the research. I laughed out loud on a lonely ward corridor and a nurse uttered 'shush' from a distant station.

* * *

I see the last few children at the clinic and wrap up some paperwork. I feel the warm handshake of an outstanding consultant who wishes me well and asks to stay in touch. I wander through hospital corridors that have an air of change. All non-consultant hospital doctors rotate this evening as 'changeover' takes place. I drop a key back to the security desk and wave the lads there good luck. Then I am finished. Out of the hospital heat. Through the cloud of cigarette smoke at the entrance. Into the clear air of the night. Another rotation is done. I can say I have met the hardest-working and most supportive registrars, the most patient, kind and knowledgeable nurses, and some of the nicest and most dedicated consultants. I hugely enjoyed spending time with children, seeing the light in their eyes and the lightness in their steps. I am so grateful to them. I feel softer and gentler from the way we have spoken to each other throughout my time here. I hope I will always be this way with every patient, no matter what age. Another rotation awaits in less than three days. All I wish for is to hold my own kids in my arms all weekend long.

13.

EVERY DAY IS UNIQUE

I pedal through streets named after boxers and saints. Every house looks the same. Row after row of identical, terraced homes. When I arrive, I look up at the pebble dash on the front of a small house and stare my fate in the face. This will be my home as a new General Practice (GP) registrar for a year. Goodbye hospital hierarchies, hello autonomy. I have completed an orientation session with my friendly GP trainer and got to grips with the computer system. It is 'day one' and I am ready to go.

There is no lightshade in the upstairs back room, just a dusty light bulb hanging awkwardly on a wire, a bit like myself. The window is wide, and I drink up a sight I have not seen in years of hospital medicine. The sky. I can actually open a window for fresh air. I gaze out across back gardens profuse with greenery. The wind turns over flushing grasses and a tree laden with red apples is almost within reach.

What is that sound? Birds singing. Nature floods this hidden suburban oasis.

I chat with the secretaries and the two practice doctors over a cuppa. I refill the kettle at the tiny sink in the tiny patient loo and place the kettle back down in its spot at a secretary's elbow by her desk. I am amazed she has never been scalded. They laugh and say I'll soon get used to the place and become like the furniture myself. The laughter and banter make the place seem bigger.

'Good luck and shoot me an instant message if you need anything', my trainer says as I wander upstairs, steaming mug of tea in hand. 'Today is unique, enjoy it', he calls after me.

Janet is my first patient and I shake her hand warmly.

'How are things?', I ask.

She tries a word, falters and her tears brim. I wonder what stresses or mood change she may be about to describe.

'I found a lump', she says. The air is sucked from the room as a pallor sweeps through her face. 'Here', she motions to the axilla by her right breast.

I search for something to say that might help in the absence of any other knowledge. 'I'm glad you've come. You're in the right place.'

We chat about her history and family. I palpate gently through the quadrants. There it is. Discrete, hard, painless. I chat in steady tones and try to dilute the tension by saying there are lots of possibilities. She does not buy it. I write notes and give her a phone number to confirm a screening appointment. After she has left, I add the question 'malignancy' to her rapid referral form. If I do not write the word 'malignancy', she will not be seen for up to six months and may die from waiting. She will still wait for up to a month this way. I am a fallible gatekeeper, writing a single word on a slip of old paper that may lead to one life path instead of another.

* * *

Bill describes getting sudden onset chest pain last night, triggered when his wife came home and said she had booked them an expensive holiday abroad. My fingers have been hovering over the emergency department referral button and now withdraw slightly.

'It's not the money', he says. 'I'm terrible afraid of flying.'

'How's the pain now?', I ask.

'Sure, that's long gone since I took one of my wife's benzos. Those are great things, can I have a few?'

His cardiac and respiratory exams are normal, and an ECG shows normal sinus rhythm.

'How about them benzos?', he asks as he makes his way to the door.

* * *

'I am trying to kick it', says Gerry. 'But every Wednesday the lads knock on my front door, and I end up using.'

'What, they just arrive and encourage you to take it? What if you told them to go away?'

'Nah, they're my friends. They come in for a cuppa and we sit around the kitchen table, talking about life and stuff. Then they start injecting. Sometimes I don't even want to, but I start into it too.'

I take my time writing a letter to an addiction clinic and chat through the process of starting methadone, which he wishes to try. I ask him to come back next Wednesday. I open a drawer to show him a collection of chocolate biscuits and a box of teabags and ask if he thinks he can convince his friends to join. He eyes the contents of the drawer doubtfully. 'They won't do it for the digestives', he says, 'but if you get a few more purple Snacks, they might.'

* * *

Mary, who is in her eighties, bumped her lower leg last week and wants to have it checked before she travels to Edinburgh to see her daughter at the weekend. She walks perfectly and has no pain. She tells me she bumped it against a coffee table and when I look at it, it seems normal.

'Do you mind if I place my fingers here?', I ask and kneel down. 'Is there any tenderness when I touch?' I know what the answers will be. I take my time. 'Let's check the warmth. Now, let's compare with the other leg. Can I check the pulse at your ankle? Can I check your blood pressure while I'm at it?'

I am not going through the motions for the sake of it. I could have come to the same conclusion in a tenth of the time and moved on to the next waiting person. But this woman has asked to be examined with earnest dignity. We take a few gentle steps on the path together and share time without rush. There is nothing more important in this moment. I reassure her and smile and wish her a lovely break in Edinburgh. She is content, her worry unhitched and left behind. That is all.

* * *

My first day is flying along. I meet people with upper respiratory viral infections, urinary tract infections, hay fever, a stye in the eye, I inject steroid into a shoulder joint and remove stitches where skin cancer once was. If both temperature and heart rate are marginally up in the context of infection, do I encourage a person towards the certain trauma of an emergency department or treat with oral antibiotics and hope my 'safety net' advice for worsening symptoms mitigates the risk of fatal sepsis? I see a mild rash causing no discomfort. I say upfront that I do not know what it is but that since they are otherwise well, we can monitor it. Coping with uncertainty is a core part of the day and I imagine it always will be. Time soothes uncertainty. I can turn a snapshot into a trend by asking someone to return. Relationships can grow with time. The surgery pit stops of a life enable knowledge of form and condition, when to act and when to sit.

* * *

Maggie has a weeping tattoo on her arm. The colours are diffused and smeared, wrapped in cling film.

'Why did you wrap it in cling film?'

'Cause I don't want it on me clothes.'

The perfect incubator. Hot, swollen, redness is seeping down her arm.

'I went to the same studio before and got an infection from that tattoo also.'

We chat about treatment and what to do if the cellulitis gets worse.

'I don't want antibiotics; I want you to fix me tattoo.'

* * *

A young mum of a five-year-old girl describes how bad her daughter's cough was all weekend. None is evident throughout the consultation and the girl's lungs sound clear. She is jumping around. The exam and mum's description do not add up, but I am happy her daughter is healthy. Just as they are leaving, mum says she is very stressed.

'I'm up in two different courts next week. I don't want to go back to cocaine again, especially as I have a hole in my septum. Can I have something to calm my nerves?'

Was this the real reason for attending, I wonder? I feel sad that her healthy girl might have been a front. I note that another doctor had prescribed anti-anxiety medication only days previously and we agree that this is sufficient. 'Ah, you're probably right', she says as she leaves. I am sadder that I have not taken the time to discuss dependency.

* * *

My interactions with the other two doctors in the practice are like those of passing trains. We signal to each other, a wave, a nod, a courtesy of standing by while we call someone at the waiting room door. But we are sole traders on separate tracks. Unless there is an agreed time to step back and reflect together or share a story, we could go from one end of the day to the other without real engagement. It could get fierce lonely fast.

My colleagues are lashing through eight-to-ten-minute consultations. I wonder if I could ever work so swiftly and still make a connection, give a person the time to tell their story, examine and agree a treatment plan. Then I recall another busy practice I had visited as a student. The doctor whom patients felt spent the most time with them was actually the doctor with the shortest average consultation time in the practice. The average time a doctor waits before interrupting a patient is eleven seconds. He waited until people finished their story, which is typically only six seconds later. He made every minute count and patients felt contentedly listened to.

I drop by a local shopping centre at lunch for a sandwich and to pick up a light shade. I am called to do a quick home visit to replace a blocked catheter. 'Bring your bike into the house before it's nicked.' The home is pristine. Photographs of beloved long-left children guide me up the stairs and into the bedroom of a gracefully aging couple. Joe's breathing is laboured, and he winces with relief when I have finished. A quick job that saves a long wait in an emergency room. I am privileged to be allowed into the sanctum of their home and witness their kindness to me and love for each other.

* * *

A beautiful three-year-old girl is under the weather. She has the classic signs of a mild viral upper respiratory tract infection. I chat with her mum about supportive treatment and the comfort of paracetamol. An alert note flashes on her daughter's file: 'check vaccinations'. I ask if they are all up to date. Her gaze drops and she says something about a

decision on the measles vaccine that she's happy with. She
has stiffened and I sense I should release the line. I carry on
with a chat about how the girl is getting on at crèche. Then
I ask if she had any more thoughts on vaccinations.

'Oh, I've listened to both sides of the debate, and we
have made up our minds.'

I feel she doesn't want to engage on the subject. I do
not want to alienate her or stumble through paternalistic
tripwires set by either of us. So, I make a pact. I say I
would be interested in hearing her thoughts and promise
to listen without judgement or comment, I would just like
to learn from her. She sighs and tells me she has watched
the *Vaxxed* documentary and that she has nothing else to
say about it. I have to keep my promise. I thank her and say
we are here if she would like to chat about this or anything
else another time. I smile at her beautiful daughter as they
leave. She had no input into the decision to remain unvac-
cinated. Should I have given away the right to respond in
an eagerness to protect the mum's independence and the
longer relationship, forsaking advocacy for the girl? Should
I have asked politely what she had heard on the other side
of 'the debate?' Should I have offered that children have
died or suffered life-changing complications from measles?
Should I have said that she has put other children at risk
because of the dynamics of herd immunity and the fact that
the vaccine does not work for some? I might have asked
her to read Roald Dahl's gentle, heart-breaking entreaty
for childhood immunisation against measles, following
the loss of his daughter Olivia to measles encephalitis. I
might have highlighted that the *Vaxxed* documentary
has been debunked and taken offline by the company

that launched it or that the researcher who fuelled the discredited information behind it has been struck off from practicing medicine. I did not do any of this. I might be better prepared in the next conversation with another parent. This time, I just asked the question and kept a promise but left a child at risk without a word.

* * *

Twenty-two-year-old Sonia grips the ends of her rolled down checked-shirt sleeves. She is anxious and says she cannot sleep. I ask her about sleeping patterns, stray into appetite, then chat about lost interests and poor concentration. Her need for sleep and an escape from suffocating desolation is palpable. I ask about any desire to self-harm. She stops fidgeting and her head bows lower than it already was. She rolls up a sleeve. Every square inch of her skin is scarred. Several lesions are open, serous fluid oozing from the yellow gaping mouths of five or six ulcers. She rolls up her other sleeve to show the same disfiguration.

'I burn myself', she says slowly, 'with a hair straightener.'

'I am so sorry you have these, they must be so sore', I say as I look closer and turn the hand over gently. 'Is there anywhere else?' I ask softly.

She unbuttons her shirt. There are several hundred deep cigarette burns across her chest. They have been sewn in neat lines, like a rough plough has traversed her heart and soul, furrow after furrow.

'It gives me comfort', she says.

'How often?'

'Every day, twice in the morning and twice in the evening.'

A self-prescription of pain. We talk. We seem to have an understanding. She is due to see her psychiatrist next Wednesday and I breathe a sigh of relief that she is connected to a service and planning to go to her next consultation. Her breathing is shallow. My own chest is tight as the transference of anxious, abbreviated breathing seeps into me.

'Can I share with you one of the greatest things I have ever learnt?' I ask.

She nods.

'It took me decades to learn how to breathe fully. Once I learnt, it has helped me through many a crisis. Put your hand on your belly. When you breathe in, fill your belly slowly and push that hand out, keep your chest still. Feel the gap between inhaling and exhaling. Think of nothing and just feel your breathing.'

She fights it, breathes quickly and puffs out her chest, straining her neck, then sighs in resignation. We stick at it, and she gradually learns. The first time she senses her hand being pushed out by her belly, she gives a tiny, astonished laugh and her eyes well. She does it again.

'It takes a little practice. Please, if you think about burning yourself this evening, will you do this instead. Make this your practice.'

She says she will. We agree on a healthy sleeping regime, and I sign a prescription.

She walks out of the room, and I feel as if a precious spirit is slipping through my fingers. Once she leaves, there is almost nothing else I can do. The moment of connection is over. I cannot sit with her as the thoughts of hurting herself sink their talons deeper. I cannot know how she suffers through the sleepless night. I can talk to my colleagues about other services. I can call in a few days perhaps to see how she is doing. But I cannot harass her with well-meaning care. This is her journey. Did I spend that twenty minutes wisely? Could I have said or done anything differently? This is a deeply fallible profession where doing our best in the moment, offering a few thoughts, a pill or two and a referral is our meagre offering in the face of the overwhelming human condition.

* * *

I crawl to the end of my first day, shattered from all the listening and a new regime. I am too dog-tired to think clearly about what I have learnt but I feel like my whole sense of life has shifted. This experience, these humbling interactions are inseparably part of who I am. The diversity of presentations has been exhilarating. Not knowing what will come through the door with every new face and darting through a head full of possibilities with the first words and signs has opened my mind. Today is unique, and so is every day. I cycle home and the wind refreshes me.

Every terraced house looks utterly different. Each with a twist of character. A slap of paint, a dash of brickwork, a colourful garden. What rich histories, generational gifts and untold stories lie behind those walls?

14.

THE LONGEST MARCH

*T*ime has stopped. Familiar boundaries that normally mark its passage have dissolved. Gone are the opening and closing of shops, the relief of a weekend at the end of a week. Movie times, restaurant sittings and doctor's appointments are all things of the past. In old time's place is a new current that captivates and carries us along. A constant stream of news and information about the virus. The most anticipated punctuation of this new flow is the daily toll of infections and death.

What I hope will shine brighter in the memory are moments of humanity that shine through the bleakness of lockdown. Precious family moments. Rediscovering the simple pleasures like treasure hunts with my daughters in the park across the street or feeling little arms clasped around my neck as I give pony-back rides at home while isolating. Neighbours I have not seen for months stopping for a chat at a social distance as if we had all the time in the world.

Strangers sharing kind smiles. People running marathons on twelve-foot balconies. Communities wrapping arms around those who need care and offering groceries and chats across the divide. We have seen the resilience of a nation in the face of uncertainty. A political leader suggests that when things are at their worst, we are at our best.

There are certain other moments that mark this passage through the lifetime of the virus for me. Some like a thud of realisation at the cusp of sleep. Some like stepping barefoot on shards of glass.

My mum and dad call to say they have coughs and temperatures. I hear the emotion in their voices. I am stunned at the possibility that they may have contracted the virus and be among the first in the country to do so. It is only days since the cogs of society stopped turning on the twelfth of March. The total number of infections in the country is less than one hundred but there is a national anxiety, bordering on panic. They had called their local GP surgery, where my mum had visited five days earlier, to find it had been closed due to virus contamination. I agree to take on their care in the hope that their caring GPs will be back in support soon.

Guidelines are changing daily, and I realise I might already have missed an opportunity to get them in the lengthening queue for a test. I dash into my surgery early the next morning, St Patrick's Day, to book a test on the secure referral system. The phone in reception rings repeatedly and echoes through the empty rooms before the line is diverted to the out-of-hours service covering for the holiday. It is the loneliest sound. Person after person waiting anxiously on the other end to tell of symptoms or seek reassurance.

All three of my GP colleagues and the practice nurse
fall ill and stay home during the next week. The remaining
receptionists and I hold an emergency meeting each
morning. We discuss how to apply the ever-morphing
guidelines and create a plan for the day. We don masks and
create an isolation room. We work every hour we have to
give. The phone is off the hook. We shift all our emphasis
and instincts from seeing patients to telephone consultations. Call after call of telling patients we are there for
them without the ability to lock eyes or grip a hand. The
language of the body is lost.

I call an extraordinary meeting of the counselling
not-for-profit social enterprise I chair. The board dials in
and I urge an immediate move to online counselling and a
stop to any face-to-face interactions. It has never been done
before and would leapfrog the public health guidelines.
There is resistance and I rue my inability to communicate the urgency better. I let the idea sink in. Within days
the executive team make this the new reality. We lose a
third of bookings overnight. We hold another meeting to
go through emergency financial management for survival.
Days later, the Department of Health selects us as the lead
provider of online consultations to all frontline healthcare
workers under stress and the general population suffering
acute anxiety from social isolation, bereavement or loss of
employment. Supporting mental health is the second front
in this pandemic and we are driven to help hold that line.

Clinical learning travels a grim path from understanding
testing criteria, to researching the limited treatment options,
to memorising palliative care medicines for disproportion-
ately affected nursing home patients.

My parents test positive. My mum recovers but my dad's fever burns on. I listen to his breathing intently at the end of a phone twice a day, like listening for static between musical phrases on a record. I bring over an oximeter. Our fingers graze on its exchange and the forbidden touch brings comfort and despair. He declines auscultation of his lungs. I don't pursue the offer, knowing that viral pneumonia or a cytokine storm would likely be silent. Rest, fluids and paracetamol remain the only treatment. The immune system does the rest and I pray it does not lose the run of itself and become a killer.

Stories trickle in from countries ahead of us on the infection curve that older people are being left on the heap as younger patients with a greater chance of survival are placed on scant ventilators. A video surfaces of corridors in a London hospital filled with body bags.

I ask for vital signs twice daily and worry that several are not settling. He is optimistic as ever, but his body temperature rages for days. My finger hovers over a hospital transfer trigger, waiting for a change in breathing to pull it. I question if I am giving the right care. Is the fear clutching my heart dulling my judgement? I call John Jumpy to run my approach by him and he encourages me to keep doing what I am doing. Most people start to feel a little better around days three or four after the onset of symptoms. He has not experienced any such reprieve. A small number may deteriorate around day seven and slip into a decline that leads to death around day twenty-one on average. The mortality rate for his age group is twenty percent – one in five will die. I do not sleep on the sixth night, or the seventh, or the eight. The fever breaks on the ninth day. I am filled with relief.

The surgery gets quieter as people stay home and the initial surge of anxious calls subside. Electronic prescriptions are a revelation. There is flexibility to get away slightly earlier in the day as my colleagues return. I dash home to mind my two young daughters and give Lisa the chance to do her work during normal hours. She has been getting up at six a.m. and going to bed at two a.m., snatching time to fulfil the demands of her job. She is the hero. I cajole the girls away from her remote working station, going through more lollipops than a children's party. We play in the spring sun at a local park. Every little thing is a wonder in their eyes. They ask why a duck does not move from its snugly nest, day after day. We wonder together. Has time stopped here too?

Just as things settle into a manageable rhythm, I get word that I am to be redeployed to a virus community assessment hub. This is where people who have tested positive at home are referred if they deteriorate. It aims to take the heat off hospital emergency departments and allow primary care surgeries to reopen to other consultations. GP registrars are redeployed without choice. I feel that basic leadership brings people along while forcing people to do things buckles morale. Despite the loss of autonomy, I am glad to be able to work in a hub to which I would have freely signed up. I say a sudden farewell to the surgery team.

Lisa helps me shear off my hair with a one blade after the girls are asleep. We have a long-needed belly laugh at the results. Patient numbers ramp up daily at the hub, but we are never overwhelmed thankfully.

The team camaraderie is wonderful. Politics are gone. Hierarchy is gone. There is positive energy and a good will in every conversation. Laughter lives. We look out for each other. Yet the hub affects everyone, each in their own way. The gregarious nurse, full of chat and smiles, mentions in passing that she has not slept properly since starting here. The quiet doctor buries his head in his phone between personal protective equipment (PPE) changes, seeking anything to distract him from the uncertainty of what the next patient will bring.

The PPE is claustrophobic and sweltering. Goggles dig into the face and eyes strain through the foggy windows. Hot breath recycles in the mask. The gowns suck hydration out of us. Everyone shrugs off the headaches. We come up for air and water every two hours.

My colleague manages an arrest of an older man who came for assessment. She is entitled to pause and consider her ethical compass. She should don an appropriate mask for an aerosol generating procedure, but none is to hand. A man lies unresponsive with no pulse. She does not think to do anything else but help him. 'One and two and three ...' echoes down the long corridor. He comes back to life after four rounds of compressions. She waits for the possible tap of symptoms on her shoulder.

It's the '57th' of March someone says. Days blur together. Time continues to collapse. It has truly stopped for hundreds of thousands of people. I listen quietly to a woman weep on the phone that no one can attend her husband's funeral that day.

They tell us the transmission rate has fallen below one and that all the containment efforts are paying off. My parents rally strongly, as do their own GPs.

Some people suggest that things will never be the same again. They feel the new ways of living and working will stay embedded where they have sunk their teeth. I despair at the thought of endemic suspicion and distancing, people crossing the road when they see a child because they consider them a vector or judging an older person for taking a stroll with freedom because all they see is the false label of vulnerability. Both ends of the age spectrum have suffered degradation. If there is change, I hope it is for greater attraction to the simple, rediscovered pleasures of life and an abandonment of unnecessary busying. In truth though, I am not convinced major changes will stick. I see the tide rush back over the defences. I see 'new norms' disappear like the ocean smoothing footprints in the sand. I believe a certain human entropy will prevail. Things seek the most comfortable state of energy in which to reside, like a perfume's scent easing its way to every corner of a room. People will fall back into old habits, not languidly but because they work. Industry may also induce us along, urging a return of shoulders to wheels of production. But entropy and industry are a small part of the story. I believe in the greater goodness of human nature: our ache for social connectedness, for human touch and warmth, for a little foolish sense of invincibility, bravery and pushing the boundaries of experience and excitement. Children will lead us back out to play and remind us of a simplicity that has always kept us grounded. We will take what we have learned and suffered and walk more firmly through challenges thrown our way, while more aware of our vulnerability. This makes us stronger.

I long for life to recover its beautiful rhythm. Will it happen? Only time will tell, when it begins again, and it will.

My daughters take me back to the park where we saw the nesting duck. The waiting has passed. Nature has nuzzled on its offspring without a care. Nothing has deflected its relent-less surge. Warm sun falls in shafts through broad leaves onto the pond. Through its dappled prints swim mother duck and seven strong, brazen and unaffected ducklings. Life brims with promise in every stroke.

15.

A SHOT OF HOPE

*W*here have all the older people been?

I pause to look down the surgery corridor and watch the over-ninety-year-olds arrive on the morning of our first vaccination clinic. Many are stooped and supported by sticks, clothes too big, moving slowly. These women and men have shaped our lives and nation. These elders and their wisdom have been hidden from sight for over a year, cocooning. They have been shielded and sheltered by their younger families for fear of harm. Some have wintered alone. They emerge from safe bubbles. The softened skin of delicate hands is released by their loved ones. They pass through the surgery door into our arms.

We have prepared for this day for months. The complex logistics are in place. Training and dry runs have been completed. The precious vials of vaccine have been handled as carefully as nitro-glycerine. Our practice manager, Anna, has placed balloons and red roses along the corridor in celebration. There is excitement now that we can help end this pandemic. Every doctor, every practice nurse and every practice manager in the entire country listened intently to guidance on a national online call just days before. This was our wartime broadcast. Every single medic was primed and eager for dispatch.

Younger eyes are brimming with tearful fear and pride. They see their parents or grandparents disappear, out of their care for the first time in a year. The first steps on the corridor are short and tentative. Every move is careful and measured. A man reaches out for air. Anna steps instinctively towards him.

'Can I link you?', he asks her.

'Of course.'

Assurance floods his steps. His feet then start to stray. They cross over and back. They lift and dip. At first it looks like a wild shuffle, or an attempt to empty his trouser legs. Then Anna sees the gleam in his eyes and starts to laugh.

'Are you dancing?'

'I am', he laughs.

They near the seating area. He offers Anna his other hand and they do a single full turn. Then he bows and takes a seat.

'I have not been out in a year. This means the world to me.'

People are chatting across the two-metre divides. Some are long-lost friends or neighbours they met daily in the park or the shops all those months ago and have not seen since.

'My grandchildren are having a special party today because I told them I was coming here. They are celebrating that they will see me soon. I have missed their hugs more than anything.'

'I still have my Christmas tree up. It's wilting a bit. But I'm leaving the presents underneath it for my grandkids until they can come. I want to see the excitement in their eyes.'

'Is that you Bobby? I'm glad you're still alive. I was wondering who was going to make it.'

As Heaney once said: 'If we can winter this one out, we can summer anywhere. We have everything to look forward to.'

The air sings with celebration.

They have dressed up. Smart jackets and hats. Shining shoes. Carefully applied make-up. It is a special occasion. Like theatre or the races or church. Some have gone to town with layers. Overcoat and blazer and cardigan and shirt and vest are all disrobed to reveal an upper arm.

We gain consent and describe rare side effects in reassuring tones. They look up in surprise once the injection is given.

'Is that it?', they wonder. 'I hardly felt a thing.'

We repeat the ritual hundreds of times. That is how a dragon is felled, one tiny jab at a time.

Goodwill and gratitude spur us on. Eyes are smiling over the brim of their facemasks. Resilience runs deep. This is the currency that will see us through to the pandemic's end and start of a renewed future.

Our legs and backs ache. We slump into chairs spaced around the emptied waiting room. The last of the older patients are leaving, happy and safe with their vaccines. The first day is done. It is the beginning of the end. We have several thousand older, vulnerable people yet to vaccinate and keep safe in the days ahead at our practice. The task feels daunting.

All weariness is lifted from our shoulders as we hear the last patient, a ninety-two-year-old man, turn to Anna as he leaves.

'You have given me a shot of hope', he says and takes a confident step into the twilight.

———————∽———————

16.

THE STRENGTH INSIDE

$\mathscr{S}$he tries to escape. Blood, dirt and broken nails prevent her getting a good grip between the bricks as she tries to scramble up the high wall in the dark. She does not think about the razor wire at the top. Something will help her. Something will carry her from the forces behind that are trying to kill her. She has to get away.

'Stop', someone shouts. 'Stop right there.'

A swarm of uniformed men with flashlights surround her. She eases herself to the ground, frightened, and stares up at the prison guards.

'You can't come in here love. You have to commit a crime to get in.'

She stumbles away from the women's prison. Down the street she hurls a bin through a shop window. She sits among the shattered glass and is still crying when the squad car arrives, knowing she is safe for a few more months.

* * *

Carrie now sits across from the prison doctor, Andrea, and me, a locum doctor, in the small consultation room. She turns a stray strand of fair hair behind her ear. She tells us how she tried to break into this women's prison that night three months ago. She tells us about the drug pushers and the debts that controlled her life on the outside. Threats and beatings came daily. She tells us about the sweats and shakes she has been having from drug withdrawal on the inside. She says she never knew addiction had a smell. The scent of neglect, stale urine, unwashed sweat and bile. She says she wants to get clean again but asks if we could just maintain her weaning dose a little bit longer, now that she is due to be released.

I ask her how the months have been. Her pale face rises up and light comes back to her eyes. She says she has earned a City & Guilds certificate in hairdressing. She dreamed of being a hairdresser as a child, she laughs, and has taken the classes seriously. This may be her path to liberty. A job on the outside awaits in a salon in a different part of the city. No one there knows where she earned her cert. She knows. She knows the long nights listening to screams from isolation cells echoing along the corridors, while cradling her knees and raging against her own detox demons. She knows the high-pitched cries of newborn babies in methadone withdrawal and the stare of toddlers who stay for the first two years of their lives and have never seen a playground. She knows every square inch of the courtyard and every hole in the courtyard netting that filtered the sky and was infiltrated by packets of cocaine glued to coins flung over the walls for other prisoners. Carrie has risen above this chaos. She has scaled her own walls of addiction, listened less to fear and chosen a different dream. That is her abiding freedom, to choose.

Carrie's time has come. She leaves her final consultation clutching her prescription. We grip hands and wish her well. Andrea turns to me when she is gone.

'I hope she makes it. Some don't get as far as the bus before scoring a drug hit. They are on a life sentence of shorter sentences. This becomes their home, their haven. I hope she's different. I'm a bit worried about how she negotiated that prescription though. But there is a passion about her. She has new skills and seems like she can't wait to use them.'

The prison offers empowering education. First words are written, and new ideas shared in small classrooms. Walls are covered in paintings and inspirational, hand-scripted quotes, like, 'be that girl who roots for the other girl, tells a stranger her hair looks amazing, her style is on fleek, and encourages other women to believe in themselves and their dreams.' There are rooms for literacy courses, school certificates, pottery-making, photography and hairdressing. There is a gym for strengthening the body.

Some choose to use all of these. Some do not or cannot.

* * *

New York's most wanted bounds in. She was arrested on an international warrant last week, wanted for grand larceny, narcotics supply, money laundering, forgery and witness intimidation.

'I want access to my private doctor. I can have him flown here. He understands me and the medications I need.'

Andrea explains that the state provides medical care in the prison.

She shouts that no one here knows the anxiety she feels. No one understands or wants to help her. If we did, we would start her on benzos.

She ran an antique bookstore and allegedly laundered millions. If her extradition comes to pass, she will get a chance to ask the authorities at Riker's Island jail for benzos, while she serves a long-term sentence.

* * *

The alarm sounds. We race up the narrow, concrete stairs. Past the padded isolation cells where women are yelling, and the small window is blanked where food has been flung. Two guards have reached the crisis cell first and a thirty-year-old woman is on the ground.

'Another seizure?', asks Andrea.

'Yeah, a grand mal one this time', the woman groans.

She is conversant in medical terms from more than two hundred presentations to her local emergency depart-ment in recent years described in her transfer letter. She has had multiple assessments and attempts to engage in therapy, but she has refused, seeking only addictive medi-cines. She has threatened, bitten, kicked and punched her medical carers. She has falsely accused them of assault. She does not have epilepsy. She does not have a diagnosis of mental illness. She has been diagnosed with mixed person-ality disorder with emotionally unstable, antisocial and histrionic traits. She is intelligent, with full capacity for decision-making.

'I asked if she was in pain during the seizure activity and she told me her tummy was sore', says a guard, making it clear that her engagement was not consistent with a real seizure.

Last month, she inserted plastic cutlery, a comb and some small mosaic tiles prized from the bathroom floor as far as her cervix, complained of vaginal bleeding and was brought to the hospital. She asked for privacy in a hospital toilet, which her accompanying guards gave her, then jumped through a first-floor window onto a car and ran naked through the car park, where she was arrested again.

We chat for a few minutes. Then she lies on her bed, lights an imaginary cigarette and tells us to feck off.

* * *

Aggravated assault; criminal damage; breach of the peace; murder; conspiracy to murder; possession of drugs for the purpose of supply, sometimes forced to smuggle them inside the body from South America; theft, sometimes stealing groceries to feed a family. The varied convictions recur. The people are different. The air of almost everyone who visits us in the consultation room is one of loss. Loss of liberty, loss of opportunity, loss of childhood. Many wounds were laid down in early years of deprivation. Their stories are complex and laced with sadness. Universal themes are poverty, violence, dysfunctional family environments, abuse and neglect of every form. Many get dental care for the first time as they never learned as children how to brush their teeth. Almost every one of the one hundred and twenty-five prisoners has a need for psychological support. There is just one part-time psychologist. She is committed and deeply caring. The compassion among all the care team is endless. But the complexity and volume of needs are overwhelming. Andrea listens carefully and with kind eyes. I wish I could help the children they once were.

Perhaps this place is an opportunity to reset, a place to launch a new growth trajectory. Have the opportunities to help these women in the tender years all been missed? Are we too late? Andrea has worked here for twenty years. She has known some of the women since their youth. She has watched them age. She understands the inheritance of crime, has visited their fathers and partners in the men's prison across the yard and their children in the children's detention centre. I ask her after the clinic if she feels the women leave here better than when they come in. Her eyes drift and weight shifts. I cannot read any sign of enthusiasm about the power of rehabilitation in her face as she thinks quietly.

There is a rap on the door. Carrie puts her head in. She is clutching all her worldly goods.

'I just wanted to say, well, thanks for listening to me all these months', she says. 'I also just got word that the bastards who were after me have all gone down. They will be old men when they get out, if ever.'

She grapples with her load and pulls out a crumpled piece of paper. She hands her prescription back to Andrea.

'I don't need this. I am ready for my new life now.'

Her head is held high.

Andrea smiles and holds her gaze. 'With the strength inside of you, you were ready long before today.'

17.

IT'S HARD TO BE INVISIBLE

*B*ill turns from the wet street into the homeless shelter. His face is red, hair wild and eyes darting. It is the first time I have met him. His voice is slurred as he says, 'I'm in a bad way doc.'

* * *

Early on Mondays, we fall out the gate from our home's wildflower front garden. Lisa and our girls turn left for school. I turn my bicycle to the right and head for the heart of town and a primary care centre for people experiencing homelessness.

The legends who manage the centre, Jimmy, Don and Sam, all shout welcomes on arrival. How they manage to keep everyone happy and on the right side of chaos is a joyful mystery. Seventy years of homeless care experience between them helps. Their upbeat energy and laughter are core to how they mind this haven in a storm. They know everyone and everything – rough sleepers, couch surfers, street fighters, life survivors, social histories, prison diaries, who's on edge, who's kicking off, how to calm the shouters, how to still the troubled, the streetwise art of sheltering the most vulnerable.

I notice quiet Michael, a social worker, who helps people safely from the streets or hostels on the day they wish to kick an addiction. He is standing by the side of a woman who is waiting to see a doctor. She is in that precarious place, reaching over the canyon between obsession and salvation. Michael has an air of solace, as if wings have unfolded from his shoulders to protect this woman from the waiting-room bedlam and voices urging her to run back to the arms of dependence.

The number of people attending our walk-in clinic keeps growing each week, reflecting the highest level of homelessness ever recorded. Health outcomes for people experiencing homelessness are significantly worse than the general population. The average age of death for people experiencing homelessness is forty-two for women and forty-six for men. Homeless people are nine times more likely to take their own life and seventeen times more likely to be victims of violence. Many long-term homeless people do not have a drug or alcohol habit but the lack of stability while homeless can lead to addiction and over half our consultations relate to this. Three-quarters of presentations relate to mental health.

A team of doctors share out the clinic days. I work Mondays alongside Fred, Mack and Brian. The inspired GP who set up the centre may drop in to help and guide. We

see up to a hundred and twenty people in a morning. They
are among the most straightforward, efficient and enjoyable
consultations I do all week.

Here is the issue. This is what I need. Can you help with
that? Turnover is fast and fulfilling. There is still plenty of
time for banter. Some consultations are quick and easy. A
prescription filled; a form signed. Others are intense and
meaningful, connections that run deep within seconds and
can imprint on each other for a day or a life perhaps.

* * *

'It's hard to be invisible', says Mary as I examine for a chronic
cough. 'It feels like people look through me on the street.
They don't see I'm just like them but out of luck.'

'I'm here for my methadone renewal but don't tell me
daughter outside I'm on it, or I won't get to see the grandkids', says Frank.

'I'm here for the methadone but don't tell me da, he'd
die', says Francesca.

'I want to get back to professional gymnastics, like at
home in Ukraine. Maybe I could teach it here', says Sofia as
I fill her regular prescription.

'My partner, Paul, died of liver failure, may he rest in
peace', says Victoria. 'We came off the heroin together, but
it was too late for him. He spent three weeks on life support,
until fourteen minutes past eleven on Friday night. He was a
strong and lovely man.'

'I'm finding the last part of the benzo detox hard', says
Andy. 'I went from the D5s to the D2s but the idea of
stopping just scares me. I won't lie, I took a few Tranax last

week. So disappointed I am. Can you give me another week to hold me?'

'My wife was shot, my parents were killed', says Ahmed. 'My ethnic minority in Sudan is being driven out. I escaped twenty-seven days ago. Thank you to your country. Please a prescription for my thyroid.'

'I'm just out after eight years', says Dano, who grips a bunch of keys so the sharp points protrude between his knuckles. 'I'm wanted by another gang. I don't know who might be waiting for me on the other side of that door. Let's have me methadone script and I'll be gone.'

'My head is caving in with the bad ideas racing through it', says Joanna. 'I had a fight with my son. I'm clean nine months but wanted to use so badly after it. So, I came here instead just to talk.'

'I made baby cots', says Gary. 'It was hard to compete with the big stores, but I guess people like the feel of hand-carved wood. My partner got cancer. I lost the business looking after her until the end. I wanted to ease the pain and started with the cannabis, then sleeping tablets, then heroin, then smoking crack – crack is the worst, it should be banned – then Roches, Xanax, Tranax with Fentanyl. Ended up sleeping in the park after the rent ran out. If you could write a letter saying I've been on the detox and making a good effort, it might help me start over and get a job.'

'When I woke this morning beside my partner', trembles Josephine, 'he was cold as stone from an overdose.'

* * *

'This work is fairly grounding', I say to Don as I pick up a new pad of methadone scripts in the office.

'It nails you to the ground', he shouts and laughs.

Refugees from poverty, mental health issues, dependence and conflict are welcome here. I have no doubt whatsoever that the people I meet will shape our future. Out of adversity comes a thirst for survival. A different way to see the world and better way to build it. But too many people are being lost for lack of support. The stories keep coming and numbers keep rising. It feels like an overwhelming tide. Sometimes it is hard to find hope.

* * *

Bill's rough hands are shaking. He holds his abdomen and rocks in the consultation room chair. I cannot imagine the demons that grip him.

'I'm in a bad way with the drink doc. I've had enough.'

'I'm glad you're here', I start. 'We can help.'

'I need the Librium', he slurs.

I want to help him. I take time to chat about how he is doing but I have to explain that we cannot start Librium while he is still drinking due to the dangers of both in his system together. I say that we can provide counselling support today and he is welcome to come back in the morning to start the detox if he has stopped drinking the night before.

Bill wheezes, 'I haven't had a drink since yesterday, please give them to me.'

I am finding it hard to believe he is dry given the stumbling walk and slurred speech. I want to help start a detox programme, but my hands are tied. Taking Librium with alcohol can cause breathing difficulties, loss of consciousness and death. It can be sold as a drug of addiction to others. I am wary. I explain again the need to stop drinking the night before we start a detox.

'I haven't drunk. I had a stroke years back. That's why my speech and balance are off.'

My eyes flit to the screen. There is no such description in his medical history list. I am about to turn back to him, face stony with conviction, when I take a quick look in the 'documents' part of his patient file. There, buried deep in old letters, is a reference to a brain infarct eight years ago.

We chat some more. His thinking seems clear. His anxiety is churning over and his body is buckled. Sweat beads glisten on his upper lip. He affirms he will not drink again today. I feel uncertain but want to believe him. We agree to start the Librium. It can temper withdrawal convulsions, deathly seizures, acidic vomiting, dripping sweat, nightmarish hallucinations, crawling skin and carry him through a suffocating, white-water torrent to the quiet pools of sobriety.

He agrees to work with the counsellor and social work services we offer, and I start to wrap up by saying, 'I'll send the Librium now to the local pharmacy where you can pick it up.'

He shakes his head. His body shivers.

'I need them now', he cries out. 'Don't you have them here?'

I am thrown back into a confusion of doubt. My sense that he is seeking a benzo hit flares up. I get defensive and retrench to suspicion. If in doubt, leave it out. I am about to close down the discussion. In thirty seconds, Bill will be outside on the wet pavement, swigging from a bottle to feed the beast wrestling him.

For some reason I will never know, this is the moment that Michael, the social worker, opens the door. He rarely calls by to ask a question or share some news. He always knocks. But today he just opens the door at this precious moment. I see Michael's open mouth through the open door. He is staring at Bill. In a single, incandescent second, he understands everything. He sees through the opaque dogma of our guidelines. He lances the fog of suspicion with a steeled beam of trust between him and Bill.

He blows away doubt and resistance with his loving words, 'Brother, I'm here for you. I can see you're in a bad way. Whatever you need to get you through, I will help you.'

Bill looks up. He looks up to Michael's face of compassion and hope and encouragement. He looks up and tears are torn from his savaged eyes. He looks up with a flicker of courageous hope for the first time in years.

Michael listens to the brief history and agrees to pick the Librium up from the local pharmacy and bring it back for Bill. He walks to him, puts an arm around him and they step to the refuge of the office. He hands him a mug of steaming tea and heads out for the medicine Bill needs to keep him safe.

Michael understands everything because he sees himself. Three years ago, he sat in that same chair, seeking the same redemption. He climbed out of his ravine and soldiered home. He still feels an undercurrent dragging him deep to desolation. He decides daily which path to choose – death spiral or ordinary life. A life of hard work for low pay, pleasures that are free and simple, twists of uncertain fate, a partner and two children where joy, annoyance, laughing and tension are all trumped by their love for each other. Through the toil and relentless temptation of a sober life, he has carried his disease like Atlas. He has endured.

All the tragedy of lost years and relationships, all the painful lessons from the past life he laid down, all the strength that has swelled through abstinence have led to this. He has reached out a hand and saved a brother's life in one breath. What greater gift.

Epilogue:
Surviving and thriving

*E*verything looks different from the sea. Every sense is heightened. Life surges from my grateful heart. My skin vibrates in the icy water. Waves lift me out of every trough and the tide carries me deeper. Sunshine glances off the sway.

I look away from where I am suspended. The sea that looks placid from the shore is a field of broken glass in every direction at eye level. The country's capital, teeming with a million workers, is a sliver in the sweeping arc of the bay, from Forty Foot to Baily Beacon. I search for the white-walled medical practice where I work and left at lunchtime, but it is lost among the homes of the seaside city village. Rising up behind the shore are those safe arms of the mountains, with their rocky outbursts, runs of deep-green forest, silver rivers that feed life to the city and peaty crests that kiss the blue sky. The hills that seem so far away in every daily task are always there, like sheltering wings.

I think of the little girl I met in those hills whom Thunder the horse saved from falling. I think of her grace and courage.

Slowly, I think of people who have changed my life and how I see it. Raj with his smiling eyes of fire and hope; Frida's quiet, wishful spirit encouraging us to love ourselves; Larry teaching self-belief in his final days; Mark bleeding out on an emergency department trolley showing kindness to his carers; Frank wrestling his black dog yet wanting to help others; Mrs Cleary thirsting for freedom in a snowstorm; the girl who cannot move playing games with her breath; the troubled woman exchanging self-burning for breathing; the ninety-year-old dancing towards a shot of hope; Carrie listening less to fear and more to dreams; Bill turning from the bottle to the eyes of compassion; and many more.

They were all dealt levelling blows in life but came back stronger. What enabled them to advance through adversity? What is this resilience?

Defining resilience is no easier than describing the human spirit. But it can be witnessed. I have seen it in the simplest of acts and words. It evokes a quiet, persistent belief that in the end, despite all challenges thrown our way, we will not only survive, but thrive.

It seems to me that the resilient people I have met addressed a purpose in their lives with a fistful of passion. Not a blissful, saccharine passion but one of grit and determination. Hard-fought, sweat inducing, earthy, bruising passion. They teach me how life is too short not to do things for which we feel passion, yet long enough to try many. Stepping off the safe path can be a liberation. I also sensed a common quiet comfort, like the constant pull on a compass needle. Many seemed at ease in their skin, in a way that suggests not only self-knowledge, but self-love. I remember the note in the petal that Frida gave me. Love yourself. This is not a gift that comes easily in a complicated life, but it can be practised and the reward is metamorphic. Love yourself and I believe everything else, including loving others and being loved, falls into place.

What we witness in life and the stories of others seeps into the core of being, what we think and say and do. Still, we get to choose. I am thankful for the choices I have been able to make and the people and experiences that have nudged me here, guiding me along this path. Without them, I would not know the best of life, my family. I would not have the peace and fulfillment of this moment. There have been knocks and these have made me stronger too. Peace and clarity come when you see things as they are.

I feel the pull and tug of currents, the wind whipping around me, taste sea salt and hear the seagulls cry. I have to head back to work. A ten-year journey of formal medical training has ended. There is always more to do. There are goals for growth and making a small dent in the world. More important than all of these, is to be the best husband, father, son, brother and friend I can be. I think of the endless work of passion yet to do as I swim for shore to begin again and feel sweetness in the unknown.

ACKNOWLEDGEMENTS

𝒯hanks to Lisa, Jennifer, Julia, my parents, John and Mary, and sisters, Sharon, Penny, Fiona and Rosalind, for their constant inspiration and love. Thanks to my wider family of Sharon, Ken, Melissa, Penny, Gavin, Jason, Emily, Fiona, Niall, Luke, Adam, Nora, Rosalind, Peter, David and Oliver for your wonderful support.

I am grateful to my amazing friends. Thanks to Kieran McDermott for suggesting Kolkata, making the trip happen and climbing mountains together; Ronan McArdle for encouraging me to go to Ghana and always being a rock; Richard Linder for wonderful conversations about resilience and making life a better place; John Langan for camaraderie throughout this medical journey; Mark Kielty for inspiring our medical footballing exploits; and John McManus for growth through adventures. Thanks to every one of my wider friends and family for timeless love and support.

Thanks to Ciarán and Gene Cassidy and all the Cassidy family, Orla Sheehan, Neetu Ahluwalia, Laura MacKenzie, Daisy Wademan, Jimmy O'Dwyer, Marie-Therese Cooney, Roman Romero-Ortuno, Declan Lyons, Susan Smith, Noel McCarthy, William Behan, Karl Kavanagh, Aisling

Ní Shúilleabháin, Shane O'Hanlon, Julie Dowsett, Owen Connolly, Mark Murphy and Austin O'Carroll for providing feedback on the writing and collaborations on medical research.

Huge thanks to Marie Murray for her kindness and belief in this book from the start, and to Eileen O'Brien and Gerry Kelly at Orpen Press for their support in steering this book through publication.

I am forever grateful to love and be loved by Lisa, Jennifer and Julia. May you always be loved. Thank you.